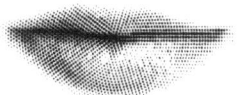

DEDICATION

For everyone who has been a source of love and support throughout this journey. Your unwavering encouragement and belief in me have inspired every word of this book. It stands as a testament to our shared connection. Thank you for believing in me.

or walk independently to doing all of that, and more by resuming her many roles, work as a speech therapist, and author of this book. This is a must-read for anyone looking to be inspired and wanting to know what a stay in the intensive care unit is like, along with its associated recovery and rehabilitation. Vanessa's story really demonstrates how love can motivate all of us to overcome the worst life has to offer, by grabbing onto the very best, that same love."

—Jessica Nobile, PhD, MSW, LCSW

"Vanessa's vulnerability throughout this book is heartbreaking. You can feel her emotions and heart break through the pages. Vanessa is nothing shy of an inspiration for SLPs, medical workers, and beyond. She truly experienced a nightmare yet pushed through and never gave up. Her story is unforgettable and will be a beautiful resource for so many."

—Ashley Reed, SLPD, CCC-SLP

"*Speechless* is a compelling and invaluable read for all! Vanessa Abraham shares a deeply personal and insightful look into how quickly life can change, highlighting the vital role of perseverance, determination, and hard work in overcoming adversity. As a clinician, I highly recommend this book to anyone who has been a patient, to providers working with patients daily, and to caregivers/family members of loved ones who are ill. It offers a patient perspective that cannot be taught in the classroom. This powerful message of hope and resilience deserves to be shared widely!"

—Danielle Torrez M.A. CCC-SLP

PRAISE FOR SPEECHLESS

"As a critical care doctor, it is an incredible experience to see through Vanessa's eyes from the other side of the hospital bed. Her unique experience as both a care provider and patient enable her to share her story in a way that provides insights for both those in healthcare and out. Vanessa's openness and vulnerability about an incredibly difficult time in her life is a rich source of insight into the challenges that patients face during and after critical illness. Her story highlights the need for ongoing work to improve care for the whole patient throughout all phases of hospitalization and recovery."

—Amy Bellinghausen, MD

"An incredibly compelling narrative of a patient and her strength and dedication to regain her life (and voice) after a challenging but mysterious medical diagnosis Her miraculous journey to recovery pulls you in as a reader, following her patient perspective as she navigates through the healthcare system. She highlights the compassion and support of those involved in her journey, but also openly illustrates the challenges within the healthcare system. You find yourself cheering for her throughout every chapter, sympathizing with her every hurdle, and proud of her every accomplishment. As a healthcare provider myself, the patient perspective was so valuable, as it's often unheard. Definite must read!"

—Jessica O'Brien, PT, DPT, CCS, CSRS

"Vanessa's recounting of her journey marks not only an imperative milestone in her own healing journey, but it also represents an important and impactful patient perspective on critical illness. Her must-read first-person account of living through a mysterious critical illness and the following arduous recovery journey is gripping, emotional, and raw reality in its truest form. It is captivating and touching, reminding us all to appreciate every small victory and gain along the way. This should be required reading for all medical professionals and trainees, as it serves to humanize this visceral, life-changing experience."

—Anna Lewis, LCSW, Social Worker, UPMC Medical Center

"*Speechless* is a profoundly moving and inspiring memoir that chronicles Vanessa's harrowing medical journey and her relentless pursuit of recovery. This book offers an intimate look into the emotional and physical challenges faced by a speech-language pathologist who becomes a patient herself, battling a rare neurological disorder. The narrative is both heart-wrenching and uplifting, showcasing Vanessa's resilience, the unwavering support of her family, and the power of community. Her story is a testament to the strength of the human spirit and the importance of hope, faith, and perseverance in the face of adversity. Readers will be captivated by the raw honesty and vulnerability with which Vanessa shares her experiences, making this book a compelling read for anyone seeking inspiration and a deeper understanding of the complexities of recovery and healing."

—Shaina Deutsch, Business Analyst

"Vanessa's words articulate what it's like to be speechless during a time critical for communication. The empathy her story evokes is one that anyone can identify with. Kudos to Vanessa for sharing intimate details of her time as a patient."

—Shannon Cotton, BSN, RN, UCSD

"*Speechless* is an inspiring story about Vanessa – a mother, a wife, a daughter, and a speech therapist who becomes devastatingly ill with Guillain-Barré Syndrome. This is a rare and serious illness that caused her to fight for her life as respiratory failure, paralysis, pain, uncertainty, and fear overwhelmed her. What makes this story remarkable is the way Vanessa faced all of her medical trauma with strength, courage, and determination that included help from her husband, parents, and medical team. Vanessa went from not being able to speak, eat, breathe,

SPEECH LESS

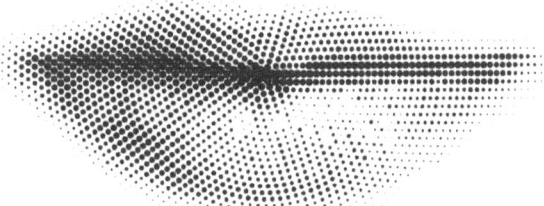

How a Speech Therapist Lost Her
Ability to Speak and Her Silent Struggle
to Reclaim Her Voice and Life

Vanessa Abraham, M.S., CCC-SLP
with Mattie Murrey, M.A., CCC-SLP

Copyright 2024 by A Neu Healing Publication. All rights reserved.
ISBN 979-8-218-54053-1

TABLE OF CONTENTS

Foreword by Jared Rosen, MD 3

Timeline 5

Preface 9

Chapter 1: A New School Year 13

Chapter 2: The Descent 19

Chapter 3: The Descent Continues 31

Chapter 4: Nurse Anxiety Increases 53

Chapter 5: Therapy Takes the Lead 67

Chapter 6: Are Those Gunshots I'm Hearing in the MRI? 91

Chapter 7: More Losses and Small Gains 111

Chapter 8: An Emotional Departure 135

Chapter 9: A Journey Through Rehabilitation and Home 147

Chapter 10: The Emotional Battle of Recovery 175

Chapter 11: Finding Strength in My Trials 193

To My Readers 217

Author's Note/Disclaimer 219

Acknowledgments 221

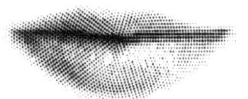

FOREWORD
by Jared Rosen, MD

In one of life's serendipitous moments, my path crossed with Vanessa's in the Spring of 2019. After completing all my graduation requirements for medical school, I opted to do an extra rotation in the Medical ICU to gain additional experience before starting my residency in Internal Medicine later that summer. We met the morning after she was transferred to our hospital for more advanced care in our ICU. This began Vanessa's journey through heartbreak, fear, courage, and resilience; this also began my unforgettable journey with Vanessa, learning the power of helping to provide care that addressed her physical and emotional health. We worked tirelessly to care for her whole being, and it was humbling and empowering to witness the profound impact of our care.

Vanessa had previously been a healthy Speech Language Pathologist leading an active life, but now suddenly stricken with a progressive unknown illness, leaving her partially paralyzed and unable to breathe without a ventilator. Little did I know that the weeks I spent caring for Vanessa would help clarify my focus as a physician and help define my journey of specializing in Pulmonary and Critical Care Medicine.

This book is a story of bewildering tragedy and suffering, but it is also the story of a patient whose spirit and unbounded strength and courage left an indelible and transformative imprint on her medical team, who felt honored to care for her.

Medicine is often framed as a one-way street—we provide care with the goal of healing our patients. Less talked about are the moments of reflection that allow us to feel the impact of some patients on our own lives. Sometimes, that's a medical student realizing that a career caring for the sickest patients who need our expertise and compassion equally allows his true calling to unfold. Similarly, a Speech-Language Pathologist might find herself imagining what she would need if she were in the place of a colleague, wondering how she would cope if she were the one lying in that bed. Or the nurse who was moved to think about what she would want if she were bedridden with limited mobility—and brought Vanessa the spa treatment in the ICU. This book is full of untold stories of how treating Vanessa not just as a patient but as a whole person helped change us all.

I invite you to reflect on how, through helping and healing others, we hold the power to inspire, transform, and heal.

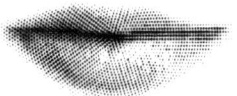

TIMELINE

- September 2018: I take an Augmentative and Alternative Communication (AAC) training class.

- March 14-17, 2019: I attend the California State Hearing Association (CSHA) convention.

- March 23, 2019: I embark on a camping adventure with my family.

- March 24, 2019: I wake up feeling sick and had to return home.

- March 31, 2019: I am admitted to the emergency room at Eisenhower Medical Center.

- April 2, 2019: I am admitted to the ICU at Eisenhower Medical Center.

- April 3, 2019: I am transferred to the University of California San Diego's (UCSD) ICU.

- April 5, 2019: I am provided with an alphabet-letter communication board by a speech pathologist.

- April 12, 2019: An endoscopy is performed, and I undergo tracheostomy surgery.

- April 14, 2019: I receive a Passy Muir Valve Evaluation & Bedside Swallow Evaluation.

- April 18, 2019: A laryngoscopy is performed bedside.
- April 22, 2019: The first Modified Barium Swallow Study (MBSS) is conducted.
- April 24, 2019: A PEG-type feeding tube is placed to meet my nutritional needs.
- April 26, 2019: I am discharged from UCSD to LTAC.
- April 30, 2019: I am decannulated at LTAC.
- May 2, 2019: I am discharged from LTAC to a rehab facility.
- May 14, 2019: The second Modified Barium Swallow Study is conducted.
- May 16, 2019: I am discharged to home.
- May 28, 2019: I return to UCSD for follow-up appointments with ENT, Neurology, and Critical Care Recovery Center.
- June 5, 2019: I attend a Speech Team meeting and connect with my team again.
- June 4, 2019: Outpatient therapy begins.
- June 6, 2019, I attended my first monthly speech team meeting at work.
- August 21, 2019: The final Modified Barium Swallow Study and FEES are conducted.
- September 9, 2019: The PEG tube was removed, and I meet my nutritional needs orally.
- November 21, 2019: I drive for the first time in eight months.
- April 2020: I return to work virtually as a school-based speech therapist during COVID-19.
- January 2025: I am growing stronger—physically, emotionally, and spiritually—every day. As I enter this next chapter of my life, I am committed to being the best mom, daughter, and wife I can be. I

am also dedicated to using my skills and experiences as a speech-language pathologist, along with the perspective and compassion I've gained as a critical care survivor, to make a meaningful impact on the world and those I have the honor to work with. My vision has evolved, and I now feel a deep calling to give back to others and help them heal. By leveraging my knowledge of the Neubie device and drawing from my personal journey, I am sharing my story through speaking engagements. My goal is to inspire, support, and guide individuals who are facing challenges similar to my own.

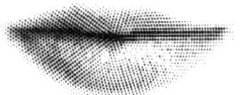

PREFACE

I was in a hallway, waiting for discharge from the ICU at the Eisenhower Medical Center. Lying on a gurney, the world around me was a blur of bright white lights. I was heavily sedated, and my mind was drifting in and out of consciousness.

I had no idea where I was going or what would come next. Voices buzzed around me like a distant radio, and I saw the outlines of medical personnel – three men and a woman – gathered around. They were here to move me, but why?

To my left, large glass doors were sliding open and closed. Each time they parted, someone entered or exited, a blur of motion and sound. I was being prepped to journey by ambulance, but – unable to speak – I had no idea where it would be taking me.

My husband, Dale, was beside me, talking with the ambulance drivers and medical staff. The presence of the woman among them brought me a small measure of comfort. Maybe she was a mother, too. Maybe she would understand my fears.

My vision flickered with images doubling and blurring. The virus was attacking my optic nerve, but I would not learn that until later. All I knew was that I could barely see, and what I did see made no sense. My husband was still talking to the medical team, and they were trying to keep me calm. They repeated over and over that they would keep me comfortable. I think somehow, they knew I was in significant pain.

Dale explained that while I was being transferred to another medical facility, he needed to go home and pack his clothes. He called my parents to tell them where I was. Moments later, my dad walked through those glass doors. I couldn't see him, but I heard his voice. It was a sound that cut through the fog. He and Dale exchanged a few words about what was happening and where I was going.

I was slipping further away from reality. When I closed my eyes, the world went black. When I opened them, it was an incomprehensible blur. The staff kept saying that they would keep me comfortable. In my mind, "comfortable" conjured up hospice. It meant I was dying. My heart raced. Anxiety clawed at me. Where was my daughter? Was she OK? If I died, who would take care of her?

My dad came to my bedside. As he held my hand, I felt the warmth and strength of his love radiating through his touch. His voice, steady yet tender, spoke words to me that were both a comfort and a plea, as if he were imparting his deepest feelings and hopes for me, wondering whether these might be his last words. Every syllable carried the weight of his love, his dreams for my family's future, and his fears for what might come.

At that moment, time seemed to stand still. Though his words were filled with worry, they were also a testament to the boundless love he had for me, a love that would continue to guide and protect me, no matter what lied ahead. I wanted so badly to tell him to take care of my daughter and to reassure him that I was going to be okay, even though I wasn't sure of that myself. I needed him to believe I would be fine and not worry. Even if I couldn't promise him the certainty of my recovery, I wanted him to hold onto hope and not let fear take over.

He left my side and called my mom, telling her to hurry. I was about to leave, but still no one had told me where I was going. Was I going to die?

My mom arrived a few minutes later, and immediately began

talking with Dale and asking him questions. She came to my side, but I couldn't see her. My vision had faded to black. The staff prepared to move me, explaining that they would keep me comfortable.

I motioned to my mom, knowing by her voice that she was there next to me. In my heart, I knew that she understood me as a mother always does. I used my left arm to move my flaccid right arm into position and mimicked cradling a baby. It was my way of telling her to take care of my daughter. "Vanessa, she's OK. We're going to take care of her," my mom reassured me. If I were to die, my husband and parents would take care of my baby. There were no better people for the job. In that instant, everything else faded away, leaving just the two of us connected by an invisible thread of love and understanding.

My gesture of rocking my baby represented my last communication attempt before they took me away. They loaded me into the ambulance, and I was unable to see or communicate. Someone touched my leg and said, "Vanessa, you're in good hands. We'll keep you comfortable." They increased the fentanyl in my IV, and I was gone. I could still hear noises around me but the bright lights were gone. I was in a void. My vision became a swirling, abstract nightmare. I saw flamenco dancers in vivid, impossible colors – yellow, pink, orange, blue – spinning around me. For two hours, these colors danced through my mind.

All I could think was, how much longer will it be until I reach the unknown place where I die? Was this how my life would end? I didn't get to say goodbye to my daughter. Here I was, in an ambulance and because of the sedation medication, I was seeing a kaleidoscope of colors, unable to talk, unable to ask questions. I didn't know where I was going. The journey seemed endless. The sirens wailed, a haunting soundtrack to my disorientation. The EMTs spoke in hushed tones, trying to keep me calm. I clung to my fading awareness, desperate for any sense of control.

Finally, we arrived at our destination, and I was transferred to a cold, metal table in a warehouse-like room, convinced that they were about to operate on me. The sedatives had led me into the waking dreams of a hypnagogic state filled with vivid colors and bright lights, although I couldn't see. The harsh fluorescent lights above cast eerie sorts of shadows and the metallic clangs of instruments echoed in the vast space. I felt exposed and vulnerable, my mind conjuring up images of a surgical theater.

Waking Up in My Second ICU

When I woke up, I was in another ICU room. The sterile white walls and beeping monitors were a stark contrast to the nightmare I had imagined. I thought to myself, "And this is how it ends." But it was just the beginning.

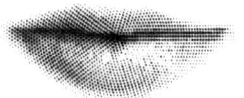

CHAPTER 1
A New School Year

The start of the school year was always bittersweet, but this year, it was especially tough. I had just returned from a blissful summer in Colorado, a stark contrast to the hectic routine I was about to dive into. As a school-based speech therapist – also known as a speech-language pathologist, speech pathologist, or SLP – my days were always very busy, and the transition from a carefree vacation to a demanding school year felt like an undeserved slap in the face.

In Colorado, I had hiked the majestic hills, pushing my daughter in her stroller, our laughter echoing in the serene landscape. We spent hours by the river, throwing rocks and basking in the sunshine. The memories of those sunlit days were still fresh, and the thought of trading that freedom for the daily grind ahead filled me with dread. When my husband wasn't working, we spent time together as a family fishing by the river, playing golf, or splashing in the pool. Life was good for all of us as we enjoyed our time together.

As I felt summer drawing to an end, I was grateful I had spent the summer focusing on my emotional and physical health. As always, I was deeply committed to maintaining a healthy lifestyle while juggling the demands of work and motherhood. I was an avid practitioner of yoga, attending weekly classes with the goal of finding relaxation and balance amidst the challenges of being a new mom. My dedication to wellness extended beyond yoga; I spent significant time in the gym exploring natural methods to manage stress and enhance my physical well-being. I was particularly drawn to organic and non-processed foods, believing firmly in their benefits for overall health. My approach to wellness was holistic, rooted in the conviction that the body possesses an inherent ability to heal itself when supported by the right nutrition and supplements.

I also made a point of incorporating healthy habits into my daily life with my daughter. I often put her in the stroller and walked to nearby grocery stores, aiming to get fresh air and be outside while modeling a healthy lifestyle for her. This routine was not only a way to stay active but also an opportunity to show her the importance of a balanced life. By integrating exercise and outdoor activities into our daily routine, I wanted to instill in her the value of physical activity, the joy of being in nature, and the significance of maintaining a healthy lifestyle. I hoped that through these experiences, she would develop an appreciation for wellness and an understanding of how daily choices impact overall health.

During the summers, this summer especially, I particularly enjoyed hiking and biking with my husband, embracing the outdoors as a source of joy and fulfillment. Being outside in nature was where I felt most at ease and happiest. Throughout my life, I had managed to avoid medications for conditions such as depression, anxiety, or chronic pain, preferring to rely on natural methods and lifestyle changes to maintain my well-being. When faced with illness, I sought out alternative healing methods, striving to avoid conventional medical treatments and relying on my faith in natural remedies and a balanced diet. This proactive and health-conscious mindset was central to my daily life, guiding my choices and shaping my approach to both physical and emotional well-being. This was a life-style approach that was about to be severely challenged.

My Typical Morning Before Life Changed

Dropping my daughter off at preschool was heart-wrenching. Every working mom grapples with a certain guilt during these goodbyes. Were it a different world and reality, I would relish staying home and nurturing her rather than going to work and providing. I never wanted to leave her side. She was thriving, so happy, and I cherished every moment of watching her grow.

Having taken graduate school courses on child development, observing her reaching developmental milestones was a joy. Her first words, her tentative steps – each moment was a treasure. Yet a working mom's guilt can cast a long shadow over these happy memories. The first day of school loomed large, and I packed her up early, my heart heavy with the impending separation. I had never left her in a stranger's care before.

I anticipated that the preschool drop-off was going to be emotional. I gave my daughter a quick hug, entrusting her to the capable hands of these amazing professionals. They were wonderful with her, and she was surprisingly adaptable for all of her 2 and a half years, but the ache in my gut as I walked away was undeniable.

My Typical Workday Before Life Changed

Arriving at my school site, I unloaded my four-wheeled cart filled with supplies for the year – therapy materials I had taken home and worked on over the summer, my laptop, and food to restock the fridge.

Much to my dismay, the elevator was broken again, a common occurrence during the previous year. This was so frustrating to me, and I thought of all the kids in wheelchairs and with impaired mobility. How were they supposed to manage? In addition to managing school, they would have to navigate a whole new level of challenges. It was infuriating that it had not been repaired properly over the summer... welcome to the realities of the public school system.

I began hauling my heavy cart up two flights of stairs. I entered my office and saw that my therapy table and chairs had been replaced with a couch and loveseat. Seriously? The day had barely started, and my patience was already wearing thin. The room was already small and working with teenagers in such tight quarters, which now lacked suitable furniture, presented significant challenges. It was both embarrassing and unprofessional to expect them to sit on a couch without the proper seating and surfaces for their goal-oriented work. What would parents think if they walked in and saw a therapist working from a couch?

In my growing frustration, I sent an email to the administration, requesting proper furniture. It would take a month for them to eventually respond and provide what I needed.

Sitting at my desk, I reviewed my caseload for the year. The numbers were high and the cases were challenging, ranging from mild to moderate disabilities to severe cases requiring complex communication devices. Over the next few months, I would meet with families in high-profile cases, advocating for their children's needs in the school system, which was always a daunting experience.

Despite my frustrations and worries, I reminded myself of my solid team. They always had my back, providing reassurance during the toughest times. Knowing I had a supportive team made the overwhelming caseload a bit more manageable. We were all working and fighting together.

Kids Who Can't Talk – An Unknown Foreshadow

The school job had its challenges – long days filled with paperwork, feelings of not making enough progress with some students, and the constant pressure to do more. I was already feeling burnt out and the school year had just begun.

As a mom, I often thought about the mothers of my students with disabilities, imagining their loss and worry. It fueled my desire to help these children, even if it was just putting a smile on their faces during a bad day.

That year, my caseload included an extremely high number of children with severe disabilities who required both low- and high-tech forms of communication. Many of the kids on my caseload were non-verbal, meaning they couldn't talk or communicate verbally. Communication was extremely challenging for them. They needed augmentative and alternative communication (AAC) systems also known as a communication device or speech-generating devices.

As a speech therapist, completing AAC evaluations was an area in which I felt less confident. My team was invited to a local conference to learn the necessary skills for these evaluations. Reluctantly, I volunteered to go. Feeling that I had no business attending due to my already overwhelming workload, I took a leap of faith and went.

The three-day conference was exhausting. On the first day, I wanted to quit. The instructor outlined what we'd be covering, including an assignment to conduct our own evaluation and write a report due later that fall – a process that would take two months. The announcement made us all want to quit. None of us had time for that.

But I made it to day two and then day three. On the third day, we were required to create our own low-tech communication device for nonverbal students. The instructor provided materials – crayons, scissors, glue, and paper – and demonstrated how to use the device. We spent hours making it and practicing how to use it on our colleagues.

As I sat there cutting out letters, coloring them, and gluing them on, I remarked to my colleague that I'd never had a student with such significant needs on my caseload that they required an eye-gaze communication device. We discussed the challenges of being unable to speak, relying solely on looking at letters on an alphabet board or blinking to communicate. We imagined the patience it would take, waiting for someone to confirm the letters before finally being able to spell out words.

The thought resonated deeply with me, as my heart broke for the student and the state they were in. I couldn't shake the overwhelming sense of empathy I felt, imagining the challenges they faced and their weight of their struggle. It was a moment that stayed with me, reminding me of the profound impact that such circumstances can have on a young life. After finishing, I tucked the completed communication device into my folder and drove home.

The next day, back at work, I filed the paper communication device away in my cabinet, thinking I'd probably never need it but keeping it just in case. And there it sat for the next six months, waiting for a day I never ever dreamed would come.

This was my reality – a constant juggling act between being a wife, a devoted mother, and a dedicated speech therapist, always striving to balance my personal and professional lives. Little did I know, the challenges ahead would push me to my limits and change my life forever.

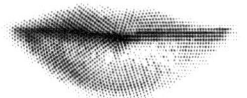

CHAPTER 2
The Descent

Six months later, I was utterly burnt out after the two-day California Speech-Language-Hearing Association Conference. The leadup had been packed with high-profile meetings and exhaustion had taken hold of me. I turned to my husband and said, "I need to get away. Spring break is coming up. Let's go camping with my parents." He agreed, and we planned a three-day weekend in the desert near Borrego Springs, California, to recharge and reconnect.

I eagerly anticipated this trip, as my relationship with my parents has always been strong, just as it is with my husband. They play an integral role in our lives, especially in my daughter's, who spends a great deal of time with them. Their involvement in her life—and ours—is a cherished part of our family dynamic.

We packed up the trailer, loaded everything we needed, and set off. My daughter was in the back seat, happily chatting away about the upcoming adventure. The drive was nerve-wracking. The desert road was rough, filled with earthquake faults, which caused the road to crack and bubble. The frequent gusty high winds often caused the loaded trailer we were pulling to sway dangerously, sometimes pulling on our truck as well. My husband gripped the steering wheel, focused and tense, while I did my best to focus on calming down our daughter and managing my own anxiety.

When we finally arrived at the campsite, my mom greeted me and brought me a glass of wine, knowing that I must've been frazzled. We settled by the campfire, trying to unwind before setting up for the night. The desert was vast and inviting, the clear blue sky stretching endlessly above us. We were glad to have arrived safely and began to relax after a tense trip.

The next day dawned bright and beautiful. We spent the day riding quads, exploring the familiar terrain of my childhood. It was a day of nostalgia and joy, sharing the experience with my daughter and creating new memories.

We stopped often, enchanted by the springtime abundance of caterpillars and wildflowers. My daughter was delighted, playing with the caterpillars and marveling at the vibrant patches of purple and yellow flowers. We took numerous photos, capturing moments that would soon become bittersweet memories. As the sun set, we gathered around the campfire, exhausted but content, sharing stories and laughter.

Unusual Symptoms

We settled into our sleeping bags early that evening, ready to call it a night. Around 4 a.m., I woke up feeling strange. I dismissed it as fatigue or too much wine and fell back asleep. But when I woke up again at 7 a.m., I knew something was wrong. Nausea and profound exhaustion had hit me like a ton of bricks. I told my husband, "I don't feel well. I need to go home now."

I walked to my parents' RV, carrying my daughter, and told them I wasn't feeling well. They took her from my arms, concern etched on their faces. Back at our trailer, I tried to help pack, but the nausea was overwhelming. Dale did most of the work as I laid down, unable to keep even water down. My head throbbed, and the simple act of standing up made the world spin.

We drove home and I collapsed into bed, unable to do much

beyond rest. By Monday morning, I was still too ill to go to work, so I called in sick. The thought of leaving my students and colleagues without notice filled me with guilt, but I couldn't muster the strength to move.

I went to work on Tuesday despite feeling absolutely horrible. I pushed myself to attend a high-profile IEP (Individualized Education Program) meeting, but I had lost my voice to whatever strange illness was overcoming me. After struggling through the meeting, I immediately returned home, completely drained. My colleagues couldn't help but comment on the irony of being an SLP without a voice, a poignant foreshadowing of things to come. Once home, I crumpled on the couch, my body shaking with nausea.

The week dragged on, each day bringing new symptoms. My voice remained breathy and raspy, and the nausea was relentless. I couldn't eat and was barely able to sip water without vomiting. Falling behind on paperwork was only adding to the stress I felt; paperwork was always a huge issue in my field. Missing even one day meant creating a backlog that took days to catch up on, impacting everything from student progress notes to upcoming evaluations. So, in the background of my worsening health, I also felt despair related to my professional duties and workload, which was piling up.

Unrelenting neck pain set in as well as stiffness. I was convinced I had whiplash from the constant vomiting and coughing. I took my daughter to school and back but struggled to keep up with basic tasks. Each trip felt like a marathon, draining every ounce of my energy.

On Saturday, almost one week later, I was still fighting nausea and extreme fatigue. I took my daughter to a friend's house for a playdate. I barely made it there, driving while wearing my pajamas and slippers with a bowl in my lap in case I vomited. The friend's mother took one look at me and urged me to go to urgent care.

As I was not able to think clearly at the time, I followed her advice and went to urgent care. When I arrived, the medical staff noticed the bowl, slippers, and pajamas I was wearing and admitted me immediately. The doctor looked at me with a perplexed expression, unsure of what might be causing my symptoms. He decided to put me on an IV of fluids to address possible dehydration, as I was severely dehydrated from excessive vomiting over the previous few days. He also noted my complaints of neck pain and provided me with a prescription for anti-nausea medication, cough medicine, and a heavy dose of pain medication to help manage the pain. No further tests were conducted at this time.

After a few hours of receiving the necessary hydration and treatment, they sent me home and forwarded the prescriptions to the pharmacist. I texted Dale to pick them up on his way home from work, as I couldn't muster the strength to do it myself. I drove back home with a bowl in my lap, feeling utterly exhausted and disheartened. I had been expecting a typical diagnosis, like severe flu or something similar, but I left with no real definitive answers as to why I was feeling the way I was. Despite the uncertainty, I felt hopeful that the prescribed medications and hydration would help me turn the corner and begin my recovery for the week ahead.

Symptoms Escalate Rapidly

That night, I went to bed early, but at 1 a.m. early Sunday morning, I woke up feeling worse. My neck was so stiff I couldn't move it. I got up, intending to lie down in the living room, but as I stood, my head tipped over to the left and I fell back on the bed. Holding my head up, I shuffled to the living room, where Dale found me, an hour later lying on the floor.

"Vanessa, you're getting worse," he said. "We need to go to the emergency room."

At 2 a.m., seven days after the symptoms of this strange illness began, my husband drove me to the hospital. The car ride was silent, the darkness and light rain matching my mood. We checked in, and I found a double-wide chair to lie down on, closing my eyes against the nausea. When I opened them, I saw everything in doubles – two clocks, two TVs, two sets of parents with a child. I mentioned it to Dale, who was immediately concerned.

I was admitted quickly, and they began running a series of tests, including a CT scan and an MRI. A doctor approached us in the hallway, papers in hand, and said, "This isn't an official diagnosis, but it looks like Multiple Sclerosis or MS."

I grabbed Dale's hand, my voice quivering. "How does this happen in a week? How do I get MS so suddenly?" Reflecting on my knowledge of neurological disorders, I knew it was impossible to be experiencing the symptoms I was experiencing with a diagnosis of MS. In my mind, I quickly dismissed this and believed wholeheartedly they misdiagnosed me.

From that point, my memory faded. A neurologist was the next physician to arrive, and dismissing the MS diagnosis, instead suggesting neuromyelitis optica (NMO) instead. "She's going to die of slow paralysis," he told Dale. The prognosis must have been shocking for him.

Despite being a man of few words, I knew Dale was very concerned because he was on top of everything I needed and what was happening. His love language was acts of service, and he showed his deep concern through his attentive care, relentless curiosity, and thorough questioning of the medical team to ensure that they provided me with the best care. I knew he was truly, deeply worried.

Hospitalization and Unanswered Questions

The disease progressed rapidly. Over the course of a few hours, my right arm grew heavy, then useless. My neck pain intensified, and my strength declined to the point where I could no longer move my right arm at all. Everything was worsening by the hour, causing the medical professionals significant concern about my future. I was spiraling downhill rapidly, which alarmed everyone. They ran more tests, including two lumbar punctures, but found nothing conclusive.

Following a process of due diligence, the doctor also tested for Guillain-Barré Syndrome (GBS) through a lumbar puncture. After examining the results, he mentioned that my feet were fine – with no nerve damage and full mobility – so they dismissed GBS as a possible diagnosis. He explained that almost all cases of GBS have symptoms of weakness of the lower limbs, not the upper limbs, so he ruled it out. At the time, this dismissal seemed like another dead end.

Speechless

By the beginning of the eighth day after the onset of my symptoms, I went into respiratory failure necessitating the placement of an endotracheal tube into my airway to help me breathe. I was then immediately moved to my first ICU. When I woke up from the procedure, I was immediately struck by the silence that enveloped me. The air that once flowed through my vocal folds, allowing me to speak, now bypassed them entirely, moving in and out through the tube that was lodged in my mouth and going down my airway. I instinctively tried to speak, to express the thoughts swirling in my mind, but nothing came out. I couldn't move my lips enough to form words and could only rely on my eyes to communicate my wants and needs.

The realization hit me hard: I, a speech therapist who had spent my career helping others find their voices, was now rendered speechless. The irony was overwhelming, and the weight of my new reality began to sink in. I had always been the one guiding other people through the process of regaining their ability to communicate, but now I was facing that challenge myself. I was the speechless speech therapist.

Lying in my bed, I was fixated on my daughter. Where was she? Was she OK? Missing out on her life was unbearable. She was the most important thing to me, and all I wanted to do was get back home and hold her little fingers in mine once again.

The tube on my lip caused ongoing problems and discomfort. The nursing staff kept having to give me lubricant for my lip because it was becoming irritated. I tried to communicate with my eyes and gestures, but the frustration of not being able to voice my thoughts was overwhelming and led to a great deal of anxiety.

Later, when I awoke, I was surrounded by my family. I saw two of their faces in the background, blurry due to my failing vision, each showing a look of profound concern. Immediately in front of me were Dale and my mom, holding my handmade Manila file folder communication device that I had crafted in that incredible difficult course six months earlier. It was the same device I never imagined needing for a student. Now to my disbelief, they were using it with me. It was brightly colored, with squares containing letters arranged on it. In the center, there was a clear cut-out for them to peek through and observe my eye gaze as I was trying to communicate. It wasn't fancy or high-tech, but it served its purpose of giving me a means of communicating.

My initial thought was, *"This isn't happening."* I could feel my hands start to shake, my mind racing with uncertainty and panic.

The device appeared blurry and I struggled to focus on each letter. Communicating with it was incredibly difficult due to my impaired vision and the laborious effort required. They asked me where my pain was. I looked at the letters for N-E-C-K, but before I could finish, I fell asleep. That was the end of using it, and I never saw it again.

The irony was bitter and stark; a tool I once struggled to create for a seemingly hypothetical scenario was now my lifeline, my only means of communicating.

Tears filled my eyes. How had they found it? I realized that Dale must have contacted one of my speech therapy colleagues. When he told her I couldn't talk, she had gathered everything she could to help me communicate nonverbally, including the device I had created months earlier.

Realizing their effort and thoughtfulness, I felt a deep surge of gratitude and emotion, overwhelmed by their determination to help me find my voice again amid this frightening silence.

Transferring to Another Hospital for a Higher Level of Care

Unable to find answers and noting that my condition was deteriorating, the medical team wisely decided I needed more advanced care and arranged for my transfer to the University of California San Diego (UCSD), a prestigious teaching hospital more than two hours away. They simply weren't able to care for my very high level of medical complexity any longer and I needed a higher level of care.

I was in a hallway, waiting for discharge from the ICU at the Eisenhower Medical Center. Lying on a gurney, the world around me was a blur of bright white lights. I was heavily sedated, and my mind was drifting in and out of consciousness.

I had no idea where I was going or what would come next. Voices buzzed around me like a distant radio, and I saw the outlines of medical personnel – three men and a woman – gathered around. They were here to move me, but why?

To my left, large glass doors were sliding open and closed. Each time they parted, someone entered or exited, a blur of motion and sound. I was being prepped to journey by ambulance, but – unable to speak – I had no idea where it would be taking me.

My husband, Dale, was beside me, talking with the ambulance drivers and medical staff. The presence of the woman among them brought me a small measure of comfort. Maybe she was a mother, too. Maybe she would understand my fears.

My vision flickered with images doubling and blurring. The virus was attacking my optic nerve, but I would not learn that until later. All

I knew was that I could barely see, and what I did see made no sense. My husband was still talking to the medical team, and they were trying to keep me calm. They repeated over and over that they would keep me comfortable. I think somehow, they knew I was in significant pain.

Dale explained that while I was being transferred to another medical facility, he needed to go home and pack his clothes. He called my parents to tell them where I was. Moments later, my dad walked through those glass doors. I couldn't see him, but I heard his voice. It was a sound that cut through the fog. He and Dale exchanged a few words about what was happening and where I was going.

I was slipping further away from reality. When I closed my eyes, the world went black. When I opened them, it was an incomprehensible blur. The staff kept saying that they would keep me comfortable. In my mind, "comfortable" conjured up hospice. It meant I was dying. My heart raced. Anxiety clawed at me. Where was my daughter? Was she OK? If I died, who would take care of her?

My dad came to my bedside. As he held my hand, I felt the warmth and strength of his love radiating through his touch. His voice, steady yet tender, spoke words to me that were both a comfort and a plea, as if he were imparting his deepest feelings and hopes for me, wondering whether these might be his last words. Every syllable carried the weight of his love, his dreams for my family's future, and his fears for what might come.

At that moment, time seemed to stand still. Though his words were filled with worry, they were also a testament to the boundless love he had for me, a love that would continue to guide and protect me, no matter what lied ahead. I wanted so badly to tell him to take care of my daughter and to reassure him that I was going to be okay, even though I wasn't sure of that myself. I needed him to believe I would be fine and not worry. Even if I couldn't promise him the certainty of my recovery, I wanted him to hold onto hope and not let fear take over.

He left my side and called my mom, telling her to hurry. I was about to leave, but still no one had told me where I was going. Was I going to die?

My mom arrived a few minutes later, and immediately began talking with Dale and asking him questions. She came to my side, but I couldn't see her. My vision had faded to black. The staff prepared to move me, explaining that they would keep me comfortable.

I motioned to my mom, knowing by her voice that she was there next to me. In my heart, I knew that she understood me as a mother always does. I used my left arm to move my flaccid right arm into position and mimicked cradling a baby. It was my way of telling her to take care of my daughter. "Vanessa, she's OK. We're going to take care of her," my mom reassured me. If I were to die, my husband and parents would take care of my baby. There were no better people for the job. In that instant, everything else faded away, leaving just the two of us connected by an invisible thread of love and understanding.

My gesture of rocking my baby represented my last communication attempt before they took me away. They loaded me into the ambulance, and I was unable to see or communicate. Someone touched my leg and said, "Vanessa, you're in good hands. We'll keep you comfortable." They increased the fentanyl in my IV for pain management and I was gone. I could still hear noises around me but the bright lights were gone. I was in a void. My vision became a swirling, abstract nightmare. I saw flamenco dancers in vivid, impossible colors – yellow, pink, orange, blue – spinning around me. For two hours, these colors danced through my mind.

All I could think was, how much longer will it be until I reach the unknown place where I die? Was this how my life would end? I didn't get to say goodbye to my daughter. Here I was, in an ambulance and because of the sedation medication, I was seeing a kaleidoscope of colors, unable to talk, unable to ask questions. I didn't know where I was going. The journey seemed endless. The sirens wailed, a haunting soundtrack to my disorientation. The EMTs spoke in hushed tones, trying to keep me calm. I clung to my fading awareness, desperate for any sense of control.

Finally, we arrived at our destination, and I was transferred to a cold, metal table in a warehouse-like room, convinced that they were about to operate on me. The sedatives had led me into the waking dreams of a hypnagogic state filled with vivid colors and bright lights, although I couldn't see. The harsh fluorescent lights above cast eerie sorts of shadows and the metallic clangs of instruments echoed in the vast space. I felt exposed and vulnerable, my mind conjuring up images of a surgical theater.

Waking Up in My Second ICU

When I woke up, I was in another ICU room. The sterile white walls and beeping monitors were a stark contrast to the nightmare I had imagined. I thought to myself, "And this is how it ends." But it was just the beginning.

As I came to, I could hear things but couldn't see anything. There were people all around me, inspecting every inch of my body, sticking things on my chest, poking at my arm, and flipping my body from side to side. I couldn't make out what they were saying. People were busy, quickly moving around me; I could hear their footsteps traveling back and forth. It was completely dark, and I opened my eyes to blackness. I wondered if this was where they took bodies that were dying. These were my final moments, I told myself. The ambulance took me to a warehouse where doctors would operate on and then dispose of my body.

Don't kill me, I pleaded in my mind. They kept rolling my body back and forth, onto my right side, then onto my left. A nurse grabbed my arm, and I could feel her wrapping something around it. I couldn't see, but I could feel it. In my mind, a bright light shone down on my naked body. It was an operating table light they were using to inspect my body before surgery. Their voices echoed off the walls of the empty, metal-sided building.

I heard a voice. He said his name was Joey. Then I recalled that before I was discharged from the previous ICU the nurses had spoken about someone named Joey who would be in San Diego when I arrived. I was confused. With all these thoughts flooding my mind, memories started to come back. Maybe Joey was a doctor who was about to cut me open. Maybe there was some miscommunication, and they thought that I was dead.

I couldn't communicate this to them verbally or with gestures, as my body wouldn't move. So, I continued to allow them to touch my body and flip me back and forth. I was totally out of control.

I could feel the nurse pick up my left arm. She gently moved it over, inserted medication, and helped me relax. I drifted off further.

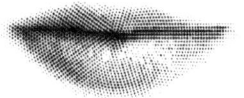

CHAPTER 3
The Descent Continues

I awoke after some time, unsure whether a few hours or days had passed. As I laid in bed my head had fallen to the right on my pillow, but I noticed I was unable to move it to a centered position. I was unable to move it at all. I opened my eyes and saw the brightness of the day.

Sunshine was streaming through my window but everything continued to look double and fuzzy. I gazed to the right and saw metal bars on my window.

They took me to jail – why jail? They took me to jail to die, I concluded in my mind. The pain in my neck was so great that I was unable to move it. My head simply fell to the right. I looked at the clock on the wall in front of me. There were two of them, so I was unable to determine the time. I saw a whiteboard to the right of the clock. Although the writing on it was blurry, I could just barely make out my husband's name and phone number.

It was still blurry as I continued to see double. I saw a tall, blonde, lean woman, approximately my age, standing by my bed. I stared at her, unable to talk. She looked at the position of my neck, unsure of what to do because of the pain it was causing me. She tried to straighten it but was hesitant. She managed to move it in alignment with my spine and the rest of my body, but my head continued to fall limply to the right.

She placed a pillow under the right side of my head to keep it upright, but once the pillow softened, my head fell to the right again. She immediately left the room and returned with a different pillow, which was not your typical fluffy, cotton pillow. The one she brought was more like modeling clay that you could shape to fit a person's head.

I watched her doubled body image move around my bed from one side to the other, attempting to figure out how to place the pillow under me without causing too much pain. The staff were uncertain about how to move my head because they were unsure why my neck could not support it.

Shannon, my nurse, introduced herself as she focused on fixing the pillow issue, and I was grateful. She called another nurse to assist. One lifted my head, and the other placed the pillow under it. They laid my head back down on the pillow. It was so stiff and hard, making things feel worse. The pillow pressed upon the base of my skull, triggering more pain. The team couldn't figure out my head and neck positioning or what to do to relieve the pain. No matter what strategy they chose, my head would fall to the right. There wasn't enough muscle strength in my neck to keep my head in alignment with the rest of my body. My neck was in a completely flaccid state.

Blink Once for No

Shannon walked over to my bedside, noticing the pain escalating and the discomfort visible through my body language as well as the tears streaming down my cheeks. Noticing I was more aware, she asked me if she could increase the sedation medication. "Blink once for no and twice for yes," she said to me.

Horror stories of others becoming addicted to pain meds after ICU stays rushed into my mind. A fear of mine was becoming addicted to pain meds, so I didn't hesitate to blink once for no more medication when she asked.

Sensing my pain escalating along with my anxiety, she tried desperately to convince me otherwise. "This will help you sleep and be more comfortable," she reassured me. Fearfully, I continued to blink once. I wasn't going to cave, even if it meant struggling through the pain and fear. The fear was real, but I didn't want medication.

As the hours slowly ticked by and the disease process continued its course and continued to paralyze me, the pain took over. I caved. The level of pain overrode my level of fear. I wanted the pain, anxiety, and horror of it all to go away.

Recalling how quickly the last dose of fentanyl had eased my pain, I finally accepted that pain medication was something I needed, not just something I wanted. The next time Shannon asked if I needed pain relief, I looked at her with tears in my eyes, gave her two blinks, and drifted back to sleep.

I woke up to the sounds of machines beeping and Dale next to me. I was relieved to see Dale, but the continuous thump, thump, thump, thump, and beeping of machines continued nonstop the entire time I was awake, elevating my anxiety. I didn't know where the sounds were coming from. Why were the machines continually making the sounds? Was this a signal to staff that I was declining? What was happening? Could they be turned off so I could sleep? I wanted to ask these things but couldn't, so angrily, I didn't even try. Shannon, seemingly reading my mind, walked over to my bedside and turned it all off.

Medical professionals, all dressed in white, kept entering my room. I was unsure who they were or what they wanted from me. I just did what I was told. They told me they wanted to take blood samples, but I was covered in tubes and unable to move my arm on my own, so they lifted it to take the samples. They always checked my wristband to be sure I was the right patient and then communicated their intentions with Dale.

I couldn't process or answer any of the questions they were asking, so I just stared at them blankly. They came and went through the curtain like it was a revolving door. I was never alone and longed for time to myself without the noises and without all the people staring at me as though I were an undiagnosed medical mystery brought in to be cut open.

In my medically imposed silence, I found myself consumed with thoughts of my daughter. I wondered where she was, who was caring for her, and how she was coping with my sudden absence.

I remembered that it was daytime, and she would be at school, hopefully playing, blissfully unaware that her mother was hanging on for dear life, fighting to come back to her and hold her once again. I had lost all control, and I knew it.

The fear inside me escalated the more I thought of her and my condition. The pain continued down my spine to my butt, but I was unable to relieve it. I was unable to move, talk, or gesture to my nurses where the pain was. There was so much I needed to tell everyone, but I couldn't. I was totally and utterly speechless.

There was something foreign lying on my lower lip, causing ongoing discomfort. All I could do way lie there and think about it. I was curious but unable to raise my arms to touch it to figure out what it was. Later I found out I was intubated, and the breathing tube was lying on my lip in a way that was causing it to blister. I wanted to shout out to my nurse to provide me with something to ease the pain on my lip, but I couldn't.

All I could do was point with my left finger up toward my lip, hoping she would be able to understand my gesture and do something to relieve the pain. The medical staff kept darting in and out of my room, asking my husband and nurse questions, and checking my alertness, but I couldn't participate in any of the conversations. They didn't know what I needed, and I couldn't tell them.

Couldn't anyone see that I needed a form of communication? Where was a speech therapist when you needed one? I knew what I needed but couldn't tell them. My paper communication device from the previous ICU was nowhere to be found.

My anxiety medication was wearing off and I started to feel my emotions and fears escalating. "Keep fighting," I'd remind myself. "Your daughter needs you back. Don't quit." But I wanted to. I was scared. The pain was real and I didn't have it in me to keep going. I couldn't communicate with them what I needed. So why continue? Why bother?

Shannon looked over at my vitals and noticed my heart rate rising and tears flowing down my cheeks, but I was unable to wipe them away. She grabbed a box of tissues and put one in my left hand for me to use on my own as she wiped my tears away with her own hand. Thankfully, she increased my medication and sent me off to sleep.

I woke up and saw Dale sitting to my left, unaware of the lapse in time. My visual world was very small, as I was still unable to rotate my neck from side to side. The muscle paralysis froze it in place, causing immense pain.

The Calm in the Storm

The curtains were pushed back and a new, unfamiliar man walked into my room wearing a white jacket, like most wore around the ICU. I was unsure of his title, but he walked over to Dale and shook hands with him. He introduced himself as Jared Rosen, a medical student who had been assigned to help with my mysterious case.

Dale immediately stood up and looked him in the eye while shaking his hand. Jared proceeded to say something about being available for only a short period of time as graduation from medical school was quickly approaching.

I may not have been able to talk, but I could certainly form opinions and thoughts in my head at this point. Really? A medical student? Where was my doctor? My anxiety elevated with fear. My next thought upon inspection of this man was, "He looks like a 15-year-old boy."

His skin was so soft and baby-like. What does he know about the medical profession, and how is he ever going to help me? Fear gripped my heart as I lied there in complete disappointment, realizing that this man had been assigned to me in an effort to help me recover.

My eyes followed Jared as he circled around my bed. He turned to my husband and started briefing him on some items discussed at rounds that morning and how they pertained to my current status.

As he stood next to my husband, I noticed they were about the same height and build, not particularly tall, but of average height for men, maybe 5'10", and on the leaner, more slender side. The only difference, I assumed, was their difference in age. Jared had short brown hair parted on the side, with large brown eyes. He was clearly attentive and absorbing all that was happening around us.

I continued to track his movements and mannerisms with my eyes, unsure if I should trust him with my life or completely dismiss him as an incompetent individual put on my medical team to monitor my case. The longer he stood in my room talking with Dale, the more I began to question my original suspicions about him. I was impressed. Other than my nurse, he was the only person who thoroughly answered our questions and took the time with us that we needed.

So many members of the previous medical team that went in and out of my room treated me as just a body lying in a bed, a job to do, a task to perform. Jared was different. His voice was kind, compassionate, and caring. When he discussed my situation and lack of diagnosis with Dale, there was something genuine about his tone, eye contact, and presentation.

His eyes and body language communicated genuine curiosity and compassion toward us both, making me dismiss the thoughts of him being unskilled. I began to see him as someone I wanted on my side, someone I hoped would never leave my room. He was someone to be trusted, and I could sense Dale felt relief having him around too.

I slowly began to let go of some of my thoughts that Jared didn't know what he was doing, although a small part of me remained skeptical out of fear. I continued to keep him under my watchful eye, hoping he would stick around and see us through to the end of this continuing nightmare.

Dale listened intently to everything Jared said, writing down notes in his notebook as he spoke about what the days ahead would look like, what tests would be done, what they were looking for, and why they were choosing these steps. As he was leaving the room he looked over at me and said he would be back again tomorrow to check in.

A huge sense of relief swept over my body because I knew he would be a good fit for Dale and would take him under his wing, which would take a load of worry off me. Dale shook Jared's hand again and thanked him for his time and help before he left the room.

I couldn't help but think of all the undivided attention and time he had just spent with us. I could sense he felt this was a unique case and we were going to need a lot of support. For that, I was grateful.

The Onset of Nurse-Induced Anxiety

The sun began to set on day one in the ICU, and I feared what was to come. Terrifying thoughts flooded my mind. I wondered what the nighttime would be like in the ICU. Would Dale have to leave? If he left, would I die? Who would be my next nurse? Would they know what I needed? How would I communicate with them?

Dale wouldn't be here to communicate for me. How would this new person know what I needed? Jared would be gone as well. I had so many questions, all causing my anxiety to increase. I had lost control and couldn't talk. I needed to get my life back, but how?

I slept in one- and two-hour segments at a time, awakened frequently by staff entering my room to check vitals or by the sounds of machines beeping. Fear and worry overcame me each time I woke up, and the nurse would strategically add another dose of Ativan to my IV, allowing me to drift back off to sleep for a few more hours.

I woke up right before the shift change. I had a crisp, stiff, white hospital sheet over my legs and plastic tubing lying all over and around me. I looked down at my feet. Someone had put a pair of bright yellow anti-slip socks on my feet during the night. Not that those would be useful, as I knew without a doubt I wasn't leaving my bed, but they were warm and provided a sense of comfort during this time.

I then felt a squeezing sensation around my legs but was unable to lift my head to see what was causing it. Instead, my eyes shifted their gaze downward. I saw something wrapped around my legs, squeezing them, but I couldn't figure out what it was for.

I felt hot but was unable to move my body to remove the compression socks I had been given. I couldn't gesture or verbalize what I needed, which sent my anxiety up, causing my heart rate to escalate again. My resting heart rate was 120 beats per minute, my nurse indicated with concern as she turned off the noises coming from my IV pole.

It was 7 a.m. which reminded me that a new nurse would be arriving soon. The hospital room was already busy with people coming in to observe me and check on how I did during the night.

The whole process of living in this hell will repeat itself. My anxiety increased over who my new nurse would be. Would they know how my head needed to be placed so I wasn't in pain? Would they know how I needed my pillow positioned so my head didn't fall to the right?

Where was Dale when I needed him? I laid there paralyzed in my bed in a complete state of grief, unable to move or communicate, needing answers, needing help, and needing a way to talk.

If I could only speak my mind and get some answers, I thought, then I would feel a little better. I would feel like a person with a future, not a body that was shriveling up and dying from some unknown disease.

I was lying there, locked in my dark thoughts, when the curtains on my left side were pushed back, and Dale entered the room. With my head frozen in place, my eyes gazed left to meet his. Despite the stress he was under, he appeared clean, dressed nicely, and ready to take on the day. I reflected on the fact that I hadn't showered in who knows how long, and momentarily felt embarrassed for how I looked and smelled. But I was relieved to have him back to advocate for me and ask the questions I couldn't.

I had no concept of time since being sedated and admitted. I looked at the whiteboard in front of me. It had a date on it, so I was able to count the days. It had been six days since I first came to the hospital, but I was still unclear as to what had transpired during those days. There was so much I couldn't remember, and I wanted to know what had happened to me.

What happened while I was sedated? I couldn't ask and the effects of the medication were so great, so my past remained a mystery to me. It's a part of my life I will never have a memory of and the loss of those days caused me to cry. I cried for the loss of what I would never know and the loss of time I missed with my daughter.

My daytime nurse, Shannon, was back again. What a relief. She was compassionate and knew me well enough at this time to know what I needed. I was somewhat at peace for the moment, knowing I had a familiar person on my side, and Dale was there. The hospital was swarming with white coats again. Although I was unable to turn my head or elevate it to look outside the room, I could hear countless voices, footsteps, and beeping machines in other rooms.

The curtains in my room were closed for privacy, so I couldn't see who was coming into my room until they were in front of me. This time, the curtain was pulled back and there stood Jared. I felt a bit of relief knowing I had Shannon, Jared, and Dale in the building for the next 10 hours.

Checking for Strength

Jared shook hands with Dale and asked him how the night had gone for both of us. As he walked to the side of my bed, I couldn't help but feel anxious, wondering what procedures the staff in white coats would want to do with me. But I remained grateful for them and all their compassion toward us.

"Hi, Vanessa. Can you do me a favor and press against my hand with your foot?" Jared asked me. Exhausted, I lifted my right leg up and pressed the ball of my foot against his hand as hard as I could in an attempt to prove to him that I was strong and not giving up. Then we proceeded to the other foot. "Your legs are strong," he commented.

He then walked up to the top right side of my bed and asked me to squeeze his fingers with my right arm. He placed his hand next to mine, knowing I was unable to lift it to meet his. I gripped his fingers and squeezed, giving it all I had because I wanted to prove to him that I cared about my future and wasn't giving up, although it may have appeared that way due to my lack of strength.

I squeezed with every last ounce of strength I had. I knew it wasn't much and I felt disappointed. I felt I had disappointed him. I was so weak, my body failed me. The pain was just too great, and the fear insurmountable to find any positivity in this.

He continued to ask me to do tasks with my right arm, completely avoiding the left. "Can you raise your arm to the side?" he asked. My eyes shifted right, and I stared blankly at him. I understood his request, but I couldn't do it and couldn't communicate that to him. My arm would not move. Tears welled up in my eyes like a puddle after a storm. I didn't want to let him down, but I felt I had.

"Can you lift your arm forward?" I stared blankly at him, speechless, feeling frustrated and discouraged at his request. I stared at him and let the tears flow more. I wanted nothing more than to do these mundane tasks for him. I wanted to relieve him of asking me to do such things and wasting his time on a person who, a week ago, could do all of this. But I couldn't, and I started to feel sorry for myself.

He proceeded to ask me to do the same tasks with my left arm, which I could do but with reduced strength. "The paralysis is only affecting your right arm and neck," he stated. "We will continue to monitor those areas in the days ahead. I'll check back in with you later today and see how you are doing." He pushed back the curtains and left the room.

Dale held my hand as I grieved. My mind was filled with new fears, and I wondered if I would ever recover from this. Would I ever move my arm again? Would I ever be able to move my head again? Would I ever be able to write, hold my child, or drive a car without my right arm? I closed my eyes and attempted to block them both out. Block out all the sounds, sights, and images that were causing me such sadness. Block it all out and go back in time to a week when life was predictable, and there was joy.

Images of my daughter arose in my mind, and I wondered what she was doing and where she was. No one knew what I was thinking or the thoughts of fear flooding my mind. I was fully aware of what was happening, but no one there understood the depth of my despair and heartache of missing my child. It was all too much to handle.

My heart rate escalated – 120, 125, 130 beats per minute. The room began to get hotter, and I couldn't figure out why. Everyone else was in sweaters and I wanted to kick these sheets off me. My IV pole kept beeping. I didn't know what it was signaling to my team, but it wouldn't stop. I couldn't roll over to see what was happening, but Shannon could interpret it all. It was my heart rate. The average resting heart rate for women my age in good health was far less than this, she indicated. My resting heart rate was now over 130.

They discussed administering more anxiety meds to calm me down. I kept my eyes fixed on the clock ahead of me, as well as the whiteboard to the right with the day's scheduled events, but my vision was still doubled. Shannon pulled the curtain to the left of me back, which, although I was unable to turn my head, gave me somewhat of a view of what was happening at the nurses' station.

I looked up at the whiteboard toward the right side of my room and looked at the calendar. A week ago, I was home and able to move, but simply feeling flu-like. Now, here I was, in the fight of my life, wondering why I couldn't move. And to make it worse, no one knew why or what my prognosis would be. Would this be my forever? Was my new normal, as a speech therapist, to be a bedridden mother without a voice?

The head of my bed was elevated, and Shannon had pillows strategically placed around my neck, head, and on my side to give my butt a much-needed break from lying on it for an extended period of time. But it continued to hurt. My lips were dried out and sore. The breathing tube resting on my lower lip was uncomfortable and irritating. I wanted it moved and needed to signal to either Dale or Shannon that I needed it adjusted because it was hurting.

I patiently waited for one of them to look at me before I used my nonparalyzed left arm to point to my lip.

Lifting my arm was not an easy task, as it was not only weak but also had all my IVs inserted into it which made it difficult to move. Covered in tubes, I had to detangle myself from it all in order to use my one good limb to point, desperately hoping they would understand what my gestures meant.

Shannon saw my gesture and indicated that she understood me by pointing to my lip. Yes!! She understood my nonverbal cries for help! She turned to the computer to the right, typed in something, and proceeded to get a lip balm for me. She rotated the breathing tube from one side of my lip to the other and gently applied the lip balm.

More White Coats

My eye gaze shifted left, and I saw a swarm of white coats standing outside my room. Shannon stepped out and gathered with them. Were they discussing me? I didn't know, but I wondered what they were talking about. What was wrong with me? Would I get better? Why were there so many of them? I counted – one, two, three, four, five, six, seven, eight – but I was unable to turn my head further around the curtain to see others. Jared was one of the professionals in the mix, but everyone else was new to me.

There were men and women of all ages, some clearly younger than I was. I reflected on the fact that I was at a teaching hospital, and many of them were learning new skills and simply doing their best to eventually take on the roles of the professionals they were shadowing.

Jared signaled to Dale to come over and join them. "Don't leave me, Dale!" I wanted to scream. "Don't leave my side! You are my voice. What if I need you?" Without realizing that I needed him, he disappeared outside the sliding glass door to the left and joined the group of white coats to advocate for me and my needs.

My neck frozen, I shifted my gaze left in hopes of seeing or hearing anything they discussed. But I didn't get any of it. They were too far away. The huddle broke up, and they all moved along. My eye gaze was fixed left, and I noticed Jared stayed next to Dale and continued to talk.

Dale, gripping his notepad and pen, quickly jotted down notes as Jared spoke. In my head, I was desperate. "Someone, please tell me what they are discussing!" I needed to ask questions and to be involved in these conversations about my care, but I felt I was being ignored. Anger and fear arose inside me and I felt so helpless.

They continued to talk for what seemed like hours, but in reality, the clock to my right slowly ticked by. Within a matter of minutes, Dale and Jared had come to my bedside. A smaller group of white coats entered my room alongside them.

"This can't be good," I thought. They introduced themselves one at a time and told me their titles: neurologist, critical care doctor, and nephrologist. They proceeded to give me a brief rundown of what they had just discussed outside my room. Initially, I was relieved to be a part of this conversation for once, but eventually, my attention span failed me.

I was not understanding their thoughts, ideas, and, most importantly, their plan to get me well again. Anxiety crept up, and all I heard was a broken record of random sounds and voices. I was sweating, but no one knew because I couldn't talk. None of their voices or words made any sense to me as my focus shifted to my daughter, my uncertain future, and the critical state I was in. They kept talking, and I hoped Dale was listening for me as I mentally disconnected.

The neurologist asked me to follow his fingers with my eyes. I did so. He asked me how many clocks I saw. I held up two fingers. He asked me how many fingers he was holding up in a variety of positions in front of me. I held up two fingers. He also proceeded to ask me to perform a variety of tasks with my right arm, but I was unable to complete them.

Feeling defeated and embarrassed at my poor performance, I just stared blankly at them, unable to properly apologize. They stated that they would continue to run tests and monitor my progress over the next few days and left, leaving Dale and Jared behind. I hoped they were going to have better news and felt a sense of disappointment from everyone, including myself.

More Tests but No More Answers

Dale and Jared stood beside me, explaining to me what would happen in the days ahead. I heard the words "sprinting," "swallow tests," "MRI," "blood work," "physical therapy," and others that were simply confusing to me, so I closed my eyes in an attempt to forget what was happening. Despite the fear of the unknown, Jared's bedside manner was calming, exceptionally kind, and compassionate. I felt secure with him delivering important news.

"Will someone just fix me and get me home to my child?" I silently begged. With a heavy heart, I observed them both, noting how polished and immaculate they appeared. Their complexions were so perfect and baby-like, they seemed untouched by the usual wear and tear of life. Tears streamed down my face. Where was my child? What did I have and what was my prognosis?

A person who had always been in control of her life now had no control at all. As I lied in bed, I realized that I needed a plan. I needed a plan for my child's care and a plan for when I would be back home and working. If only I could talk.

If I were going to die of paralysis, I needed to know so that I could make sure my child was OK. I wanted medication so I could sleep and not think, but they wouldn't give me any more.

They discussed ICU delirium with me and the reasons why they didn't want me sleeping during the day. I wanted something to take me away but couldn't sleep with all the foot traffic, blaring noises of ventilators, and incessant beeping of machines. My eyes shifted right, looking at the clock – it was 7 p.m. This meant a new shift was coming on, and that meant that I had to train someone new.

I knew Shannon had to leave at some point to go home to her own family. What would happen when she left? I kept wondering, and more importantly, who would be my voice when Dale left? Who would come next? How would they know how my neck and head needed to be positioned? What about my butt? It was in such pain. How would this next person know what I needed? Complete panic set in with each new transition. All I could do was cry.

Without asking a question, Shannon left the room and came back with something to help me. Later, I realized she was slowly feeding me little boluses of Ativan medication to calm my anxiety.

Anxiety had become a new state for me as, prior to this week, I had never considered myself an overly anxious person. Immediately, the sedative took over, and I felt a little more at ease as I closed my eyes and tried to block out the beeping sounds and blaring trumpet-like noises of ventilators in the background.

It was all medically necessary life-saving equipment. Nonetheless, that equipment made it difficult to relax and sleep. I was never sure whether it was my machine or someone else's, further increasing my anxiety. I often wondered if these sounds indicated someone was dying and wondered if one day it would be me.

Dale stepped outside the sliding door to my left and headed to the nurses' station. My eye gaze darted left, carefully watching every step he took and curiously wondering what he was saying to each person he talked to, but I was unable to see much. Within minutes, he returned to tell me I'd have a new night nurse. Her name was Andy. Panic set in – a new nurse was not good. A new person would need to be trained, and I couldn't talk to train her.

Unable to talk back, I just blankly stared. A blank stare was my only form of communication. At this point, I was fully aware of what was happening and what a new nurse entailed. Being aware of everything had its drawbacks because, as a patient, you are aware of the magnitude of what's unfolding, and for me, knowing I had a new nurse who didn't know my case was just as bad as not knowing what was wrong with me.

However, I knew there was nothing I could do about it, and I had to give up control and let them do what they did best. I reminded myself of this over and over again in hopes it would relax and reassure me. It didn't work, and my mind and fears raced on. At this point, it was my mind against me.

The new nurse, Andy, entered my room and approached my bedside. She possessed an eager smile and a fighting spirit. "I am your night nurse," she told me. "If you need anything, I will be here."

She saw that my head had fallen to the right. Dale immediately stepped in and showed her how I liked it adjusted. Dale explained to her how it falls to the right and that I am unable to move it forward from that position. He explained how staff had recently made pillow rolls with towels and tucked them against the sides of my head to prevent it from falling over. He demonstrated how to do it and how they towels should be placed under each side of my head to keep it in alignment.

Andy took the time to explain the course of events for the evening – medication and a quick wipe down, which constituted my bath. It was nearly 8 p.m. by the time this process began. Doing the math in my head, I knew there was no way I was getting to sleep before 10 p.m.

Remembering that sleep was crucial, I became anxious, wondering how I'd ever get enough sleep to begin my healing journey. More anxiety slammed my body. Worry consumed me; if it wasn't one thing, it was another. Andy made sure I had my call button nearby before leaving the room in case I needed her.

I knew Dale needed to leave soon, too, which further exacerbated my anxiety. He couldn't sleep there, and I knew he needed to sleep as well. I lied there wondering where my child was and what was she doing. I had no idea, but nonetheless, I wondered and worried about my loved ones. I remembered that she was with my parents and that she was safe and loved, but I had no idea what she was thinking or what others were telling her about her mom's state of health.

No one knew my child like I did, and I wanted to scream at everyone around me that she needed me, and I needed to go home, but I couldn't make a sound. A daughter needs her mother at this age, and not knowing what was happening to my body was tearing me apart. I had lost all control. I was locked in this place with bars on the windows. It felt like a prison, and I was trapped. I longed to hold my daughter next to me and fall asleep.

Dale approached my bed and said he was going to leave for the night. I knew that was coming but was hoping that somehow, he was going to stay instead. Transitions nearly killed me each time, and I felt I needed to be medicated to deal with this process. He kissed my forehead and walked out, leaving me alone in the dark room. I knew I was going to lose my mind without something to relieve the panic brewing inside me, so I hit my call button and Andy appeared.

In the Stillness: Alone with the Night Staff

Andy put something into my IV to relax me, and I fell asleep, but not without interruptions. The frequent blaring of ventilators, nursing staff on their rounds, and respiratory therapists coming in to check on my status woke me each time. I would sleep for a few hours, then wake in a panic and hit the call button.

Andy would immediately pick up the other end and, within seconds, be in my room, ready to ask a series of yes/no questions. "Are you OK?" she asked. I gestured thumbs down. Are you having a hard time sleeping? I gestured thumbs up. "You will be ready for your next round of medication soon, so let me go get it. That should help you relax and get back to sleep." Good.

She understood my needs and I could now disconnect from the world and go to sleep. She came back, inserted more Ativan into my IV, and I drifted off into slumber.

I woke up a few hours later, knowing it was another day I had to face. I could see the sun starting to peek through the bars on the windows to my right. I looked at the clock – 4 a.m. I wanted to go back to sleep so I didn't have to think about anything, but my mind couldn't stop anticipating the events of the day ahead, so I lied there, uncomfortable and awake.

I pushed my call button and Andy came in. To communicate that I needed to be adjusted in bed, I learned to use my left hand by motioning a thumbs-up sign up and down to indicate I needed to be pulled up in bed. Unable to move me on her own, she called for backup, and two nurses immediately appeared.

They gripped the sheets under me, and on the count of three, they pulled me back up, stood back, and quickly noticed my head fell to the right as it always did without support. They tucked the towel rolls under the sides of my head and fluffed up the pillows under my sides.

I gave them a thumbs up signaling that I was OK or at least

comfortable. In my mind, I was not OK by any stretch of the imagination, but I was comfortable for the time being.

As the sun rose in the ICU, the noise rose as well. I looked left out the sliding glass doors and saw a new shift of nurses arriving and conversing with the night staff. I wondered who would be assigned to care for me. I hoped Shannon was back. I needed someone who understood my complex needs, and I worried about what would happen if someone unfamiliar took over.

I heard the door slide open and my eyes darted left. Dale was walking in wearing the same light blue sweatshirt he had on the previous day. I wondered if he had slept well or showered, but I couldn't ask, so the thought dissipated. It really didn't matter at this point. I was just relieved he was there and hadn't given up hope.

"I'm going to the nurses' station to see if I can find out who your nurse is for the day. I'll be right back," he said. My eye gaze followed him out the door as he looked at the wall listing the day's schedule. He walked over to Andy, and I assumed he was looking for a recap of the night. I wanted to be the one discussing my life, but I wasn't, so I continued to lie tethered to my bed by the machines and tubes keeping me alive.

My eye gaze shifted left as I heard the curtains pull back. Dale and Jared entered the room, both looking clean, focused and prepared to take on the day ahead. I continued to wonder what I looked like under all these tubes. The days blurred together, and I couldn't recall the last real shower I took.

Jared proceeded to say something about my anxiety at night and his concerns about both my lack of sleep and my constant need for medication to go to sleep, but I couldn't focus on his words. I heard sounds coming from his mouth, but his words didn't have much meaning to me. The fear of my situation crippled me to the point of being unable to comprehend language. I closed my eyes, completely ignoring the rest of his conversation, and hoping he would just leave me alone.

I opened my eyes a minute later to see him still standing at the foot of my bed. With a combination of gratitude and anger flowing inside me, I looked at him. His morning neuro exam was part of his routine with me each day. Knowing that was what was next, I raised my foot and angrily pushed against his hand with as much force as I possibly could. My goal was to communicate to him with the strength of my legs how angry I was. My feet were definitely the strongest part of my body, he indicated once again. Then he proceeded around toward my right side. "Squeeze my finger," he said.

I wanted to rip his finger off but lacked the strength. So instead, I gently wrapped my fingers around his and squeezed, knowing I wasn't strong enough to kill a fly. I felt discouraged and embarrassed. He held his hand in front of mine, indicating to me that he wanted to see if I could reach forward and touch his.

The last part of the exam was to raise my right arm to the side. I tried and tried again, but it wouldn't move. I wanted to impress him and not let him down, so I used my left hand to encourage it to move outward. It felt heavy, but the only way I was going to get it to move was with a maximum of assistance. I looked at both of them, shrugged my shoulders, and started to cry. I felt embarrassed and disappointed as I hoped I would have been able to do more since the day before, but there was zero progress.

I closed my eyes as tears slowly dripped down my face. My head fell to the right, causing pain, but I simply didn't care. However, they did. They both reached for the towels, rolled them back up, and tucked them under my head for support. I was grateful but couldn't help thinking I wished I were dead, and someone would pull the plug from these machines that were keeping me alive.

I didn't want to live if this was my outcome. I closed my eyes for a few moments hoping they would just leave so I could have a few minutes alone to reflect, but they didn't. I opened my eyes to see Dale and Jared standing at the foot of my bed, looking at the blank white wall in front of me. What were they doing? I could only wonder and watch.

A Mosaic of Family Moments

Dale was holding a stack of white papers and Jared was holding a roll of tape. Dale grabbed a chair and stood on it. This was certainly uncharacteristic for both of them, but I continued to watch. Jared gave Dale a piece of tape, and he proceeded to tape a picture on the wall. My vision wasn't perfect, but I immediately recognized that the pictures being hung one after another were pictures of my daughter.

The photos included some from our camping trip just over a week prior, along with many others. The white walls were now transformed into a mosaic of pictures for everyone to look at when they entered. As I watched the two of them working as a team to help lift my spirits and take a leap of faith to keep me motivated, my heart sank and I started to cry, even while I also deeply appreciated their efforts. I missed my daughter so much and wanted to go back in time and hold her again like I did when I was well. As much as I loved the new wallpaper in my room it also made my heart hurt for the time I was losing with her. Their mosaic was a double-edged masterpiece.

Dale knew how much I missed our daughter and did his best to console me in his own way. For a man of few words who often struggled to show emotion, this gesture spoke volumes. His concern and love were evident in every carefully placed photo, a silent yet powerful way of expressing his support and urging me to stay strong and keep fighting.

As if on cue, I noticed the swarm of white coats filtering through the halls as part of their usual medical rounds routine. They stayed outside my door, peering in as they huddled together and discussed my medical status and the mystery I continued to be for them.

When they were done with their team rounds, they all entered my room. I wasn't sure how they all managed to fit in the small, rectangular-shaped room filled with life-saving machines. However, they packed in and conducted their own version of a neuro exam.

They began by checking my vision again, as that was a continual concern for them. I looked up. There were two clocks. The neurologist held his fingers in a variety of locations, and I saw two again. I held up two fingers to indicate two objects, failing this exam once again.

The neurologist looked over at Dale and walked close to him. "We really don't know what's going on," he said. "We can speculate as to what's happening, but we don't have a cause or definitive diagnosis. We want to run more tests. She needs another brain scan and another lumbar puncture."

"What do you think it could be?" Dale asked him.

"We think it could be a variety of things, but we won't know until we do more tests. We're currently sending blood work to the Centers for Disease Control and Mayo Clinic for review. There are a lot of neurological diseases that can lead to paralysis, which we know is happening here. But we also know the previous hospital tested for things such as botulism, myasthenia gravis, MS, neuromyelitis optica, and Guillain-Barré Syndrome. While some of those seem like likely diagnoses, they still don't explain all of her particular symptoms. For now, we need further tests and want to get started with PT, OT, and speech therapy in order to help her with her mobility and assess her communication and swallow functions."

The doctors then left, leaving Dale and me alone in my room to reflect. This was a huge critical conversation with no specific outcomes. That was a reason for concern. And I was speechless, in an ICU bed.

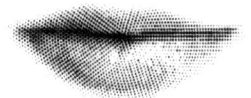

CHAPTER 4
Nurse Anxiety Increases

It was morning, and I woke up to an ICU bustling with the sounds of shift change. The low hum of voices, the beeping of machines, and the shuffle of footsteps filled the air. I turned to my right and saw the sun peeking through the bars on the windows, casting a gentle glow across the room.

"Shannon is on vacation," I overheard someone say. Darn. I recall the conversation in which Dale mentioned Shannon's trip to, oddly enough, my hometown. Although the staff tried their best to ensure that I would have the same nurse each day, my anxiety increased at the thought of having to train yet another new person. The uncertainty of new faces brought a fresh wave of stress.

Each day, my room became more adorned with cards, family photos on the walls, and colorful balloons. These tokens were meant to motivate me and show support, making me feel cared for. While these gestures from friends and family were touching, I couldn't shake the feeling that their impact would eventually fade as their lives returned to normal and mine progressed through the rehabilitation journey.

As I lied there, absorbing the morning's activity, I heard Dale's familiar voice in the distance. It must be around 7 a.m., the start of a new shift and another day of facing the unknown.

I assume he's checking in at the nurses' station and asking the usual questions: "How was her night?" "What was on her schedule for the day?" and, knowing Shannon was on vacation, "Who was lined up to be her nurse for the day?" He knew my nurse anxiety was always high.

The curtains pulled back, and there he was with his bright-eyed look and positive demeanor. His presence brought a fleeting sense of normalcy to the sterile room. I noticed how polished and well-groomed everyone else looked – clean-shaven, fresh-faced, and neat. In contrast, I couldn't help but speculate on how disheveled and unkempt I must have appeared. I glanced down at my nails, the once-pink manicure from weeks ago had now grown out, chipped and neglected. I attempted to move the blanket from my legs but found myself too weak. I could only imagine the long, unshaven hairs that must be covering them.

My hair was pulled up in a bun, and though I didn't remember how it got that way, I was grateful it was out of my face. But the thought of eventually having to brush through it filled me with dread. How long had it been since it was last washed? A week or two, maybe more. I couldn't be sure. The uncertainty gnawed at me.

I felt trapped in this body, unable to speak, a helpless, voiceless person with a face, a name, and an unknown progressive disease. The realization washed over me, intensifying my sense of isolation and vulnerability. I was acutely aware of my dependency on others for even the simplest tasks, and the frustration of not being able to communicate my needs or fears only added to my growing despair.

The activity in the ICU heightened as morning rounds began. The group of white coats stood outside my room like a swarm of buzzing bees. I gazed left to see them periodically glance my way as they discussed my care. They ended their rounds and all went their separate ways, except Jared.

I could see him turn to look at Dale through the sliding glass door. His expression was a sign of compassion and friendship, yet with a hint of sadness – sadness for our family and the devastation this disease had brought. In my mind, I couldn't help but think that his kindness and baby-like, youthful skin brought me back in time.

Seeing them together brought me comfort. The similarities in their postures and demeanor were reassuring to me, but at the same time, they added to my guilt – guilt at interrupting their lives and at having them assist a perfectly healthy woman who statistically should not have been here.

"She's healthy. Why is there sudden-onset paralysis?" I heard Dale ask him. This was not one of those situations where you'd expect a person to go down and out with a horrific medical diagnosis. I was, after all, a very healthy, young, active individual. They turned into my room.

My heart rate monitor beeped loudly, its piercing sound cutting through the room and jolting my already frayed nerves. Jared's attention snapped to the monitor, and he quickly pushed a few buttons, silencing the alarm. My heart raced even faster, anxiety coursing through me like a tidal wave.

"What does all that mean?" Dale asked, his voice tinged with concern.

"It beeps when her heart rate rises, and right now, it's significantly elevated. She's extremely anxious and stressed," Jared explained, his voice also concerned as he glanced back at the monitor.

Inside My Head I'm Screaming

Tears welled up in my eyes, blurring my vision. Inside, I was screaming, "Well, what do you expect? I'm a mom in the ICU, and no one knows why I'm here!" The weight of my unspoken words hung in the air as both men looked at me, their expressions a mix of worry and helplessness. I looked back at them, feeling the pressure of the moment crush me.

An uncomfortable silence settled over the room, making my anxiety spike even higher. What's next? Why isn't anyone saying anything? I wished someone would answer my questions, hold my hand and tell me I would be ok. This would have decreased my fears. But no one did. No one could. The silence was deafening, and I wanted to scream for someone to speak. But I couldn't. The breathing tube wedged between my vocal cords kept me voiceless and speechless, unable to shatter the silence.

Jared finally spoke, breaking the oppressive quiet. "Vanessa, we've sent your blood samples to the Mayo Clinic and the CDC, and they haven't found anything definitive. They're exploring the possibility of an enterovirus," he explained, his tone somber. "But beyond that, we don't have any answers for you."

The words hung in the air, heavy and suffocating. The room felt like it was closing in on me. I wanted to cry out in frustration, to demand answers, but I was trapped in this silent nightmare. Jared's eyes met mine, filled with a mixture of empathy and helplessness. Dale shifted uncomfortably, his concern palpable as he squeezed my hand gently, trying to offer some semblance of comfort.

I stared blankly at both of them, offering a weak thumbs up to signal with my left hand that I understood and heard their explanations. However, deep down, I was desperate to know my prognosis. I yearned to understand what my future held and whether this uncertainty and suffering would be my new reality forever.

Jared began outlining the plan for the day with a calm, reassuring tone. "The medical rehab team will be conducting their initial assessments today. The physical and occupational therapy teams will evaluate your mobility and your ability to manage daily activities." As he spoke, a wave of apprehension washed over me.

The very thought of physical and occupational therapy felt overwhelming. Yet, deep down, I knew that I needed to start moving, to get out of bed, if I was ever going to make progress and regain some semblance of normalcy.

"Speech therapy is also part of the rehab team," Jared continued, his voice steady but empathetic. "First, they'll assess your communication abilities and later, when you are no longer orally intubated, they'll assess your swallowing abilities and determine how safe it is for you to eat and drink." As he mentioned speech therapy, my anxiety spiked again.

The idea of being evaluated for communication and swallowing, basic functions I had always taken for granted, filled me with despair. The pressure of facing yet another aspect of my condition weighed heavily on me.

My mind raced with questions about each therapy's implications. Would I be able to move again like I used to? How would I manage daily tasks on my own? The prospect of speech therapy, while necessary, added another layer of uncertainty. The realization that every aspect of my life was under scrutiny amplified my anxiety. I felt trapped between the need to face these evaluations and the fear of what they might reveal about my future.

A wave of heat suddenly overwhelmed me, and I started to sweat profusely. I pointed to the blankets on my legs and tried to wiggle my feet as much as I could, signaling that I needed them removed. The heat was unbearable, and although I wanted to scream for relief, I couldn't. Instead, I used my left finger to point to my blanket and used the strength of my legs to push the sheets away. Sensing the urgency in my gestures, they swiftly removed the blankets from my legs.

"Do you want the fan on?" Dale asked. I gave a quick thumbs up in response. The room felt stiflingly hot, and I couldn't understand why he was still wearing a sweatshirt.

As they continued to talk, all I could think about was my child growing up without me. Images of her hitting developmental milestones without my encouragement – starting school, learning to ride a bike, and growing up – flashed through my mind like a relentless nightmare. The thought of her experiencing these moments without me by her side was overwhelming. How would my husband manage to raise her alone?

I couldn't focus on what was being said around me. I shifted my gaze back to the wall in front of me, my wall of motivation. It was covered with images of me and my daughter, plastered like wallpaper.

Those pictures were my lifeline, a visual reminder of why I needed to keep fighting and find the strength to press on.

As the conversation continued, I caught fragments of words like "swallow study," "additional brain MRI," "sprinting," and "walk." The mention of "sprinting" was baffling – I couldn't even walk, let alone sprint. What on earth were they talking about?

The sounds of the ICU dominated my senses – the steady thumping of my ventilator, the beeping of my heart rate monitor, and the discordant noises of other patients' equipment. The clamor was tremendous, drowning out everyone else and leaving me with only the harsh, insistent noises of the hospital environment.

I glanced at the clock. It read 9:15. I mentally counted down the hours until 8 p.m., when I knew I could finally end another grueling day and go to sleep. I looked down at my lap and saw a tangled web of dark, endless tubes snaking across my body. Some were inserted into my arms, while others led to various machines. The sight of them was overwhelming – I didn't fully understand their purposes, but they were everywhere, and their weight felt like an oppressive burden, dragging down my arms and adding to my sense of helplessness.

I looked at Dale and gave him the thumbs-over-my-shoulder signal, a silent plea for help in repositioning myself. Understanding the urgency, he stepped out to find assistance. Within moments, my new nurse, Rachel, arrived. She was young, with light brown hair, and spoke in a soft, gentle, and reassuring tone. Quickly assessing the situation, her expression mirrored the seriousness of my condition. She introduced herself and reassured me that she would get some help to reposition me and make me comfortable again, explaining each step so I would know what to expect. There was something about Rachel that calmed my anxiety, allowing me to focus on her words instead of my fears.

Dale introduced himself to Rachel and immediately began to educate her about my specific needs. He explained how I required the towels to be rolled up and strategically placed behind my head and around my neck for optimal comfort. His familiarity with my care routine and his presence provided a small but significant sense of reassurance.

The clock now read 10:15 – another hour had passed. The curtain to the left was pulled open, and my gaze shifted accordingly, eager to catch a glimpse of who it might be. It was another medical professional, dressed in a crisp white coat. She looked unfamiliar, yet there was an air of professionalism and competence about her appearance.

Meeting the Speech Pathologist

The woman spoke. "Hi, my name is Danielle. I'm a speech pathologist." Her voice was articulate and professional, conveying immense knowledge as she got straight to the point. This was the moment I had been waiting for, but also the one I could live without. This bad dream was, in fact, my reality. I was also a speech pathologist, a speechless speech pathologist at that, and now there was a speech pathologist standing in front of me, assessing me.

Fighting back tears, I couldn't help but wonder what she was thinking. Was she nervous about working with a colleague? Was she as concerned and as sad as I was? She was about to face a challenge that grad school or clinical experience had never prepared her for.

I looked at her hoping that, colleague to colleague, she could understand my nonverbal stares. We were experts in communication, right? She should be able to fix this in no time. "Please help me talk. You understand me and my communication needs more than anyone," I desperately wanted to tell her.

I noticed she had a stack of papers, each neatly enclosed in plastic sleeves. She handed them to me and explained that they were for communication. I gave her a thumbs up, signaling that I understood. She assisted me in flipping through the pages. The first was an alphabet board filled with letters, and the subsequent pages had images to point to. I gripped these pages tightly; they were my lifeline to others. They were my voice. My voice.

Despite the overwhelming fear of not being able to speak, I found a small sense of relief as I looked at the communication aids in my hands. Now I could ask questions that had been haunting me. I could find out how my child was doing, something I'd been desperate to know. I could ask about my prognosis, something I'd been too terrified to voice.

These pages offered me a way to express my concerns and anxieties, a way to communicate what had been building up inside me for days. I held the communication pages tightly, feeling a mix of newfound hope and profound sadness as I came to terms with being an official AAC user. The reality of my situation had settled in, but with these pages in hand, I could start asking the questions that had been pressing on my mind.

Danielle looked sympathetically at Dale and instructed him to page her if he needed anything, ensuring that he knew how to reach her quickly. Her confidence and reassurance made me certain that I was in good hands with this team. They truly understood my needs. As she turned to leave, she gently closed the curtain behind her, giving Dale and me a moment of privacy.

I gripped my communication pages tightly, feeling their importance more than ever, and began asking the questions that had been weighing on my mind.

With trembling fingers, I carefully pulled the papers onto my lap and begin the painstaking process of finger-spelling. Each movement was deliberate and slow, requiring immense concentration and effort as I slowly spelled out words letter by letter. The task was laborious and exhausting, but it was my only means of communication, and I focused intently on each letter, determined to convey my thoughts despite the emotional fear of knowing the answers to all my burning questions.

I painstakingly typed out our daughter's name. Dale restated it aloud to be sure he had understood, and I gave a thumbs up. "She's with your parents. They're taking great care of her. They're making sure she goes to school, and she's doing well and is very loved by them. Try not to worry about that, Vanessa," he said. While this knowledge provided some comfort, it didn't erase the profound sadness of being separated from my child.

I couldn't think of anyone else in the world who could care for her with the same love and dedication as my parents. She had always had a special bond with them and their unwavering support made me believe she was in the best hands possible. Still, knowing they were giving her the same warmth and attention I would didn't completely alleviate the heartache.

The thought of being apart from her weighed heavily on me. Missing out on her daily life and milestones and holding her close was agonizing. The deep longing to be with her was a constant ache, fueling my determination to heal and return to the life I was desperately missing.

I pointed to the letters N-E-C-K, each slowly and individually, as I became accustomed to communicating with the alphabet board. "Do you need it adjusted?" Dale asked. I flipped the pages and found Y-E-S.

He retrieved the towel, carefully repositioning my head to alleviate the pain that was exacerbated by improper alignment. As he adjusted it, I flipped back to the front page of the alphabet board, slowly and deliberately touching the letters L-U-B-E, indicating that my lips were hurting and needed ointment. The blisters were causing significant discomfort.

Rachel, who had been typing at the computer a few feet away, turned and approached my bedside. Her eyes, filled with compassion, silently reassured me that she was there to help. Attentive to my needs, she quickly returned with the requested relief. I then spelled out M-O-V-E, and pointed to my mouth, hoping to convey that the object causing the irritation needed to be moved.

She carefully adjusted the piece on my lip and applied a soothing, jelly-like ointment. "Is there anything else you need?" she asked gently. I typed out N-O to signal no additional needs, followed by T-H-A-N-K-Y-O-U.

I wanted to show kindness to the staff, making extra efforts to be polite and appreciative so they would know I valued their care. Reflecting on my own experiences as a speech therapist, I remembered how much it meant to me when families were genuinely kind and grateful. Their appreciation often motivated me to go the extra mile in providing the best care possible. I hoped that by being considerate and acknowledging their efforts, I could foster a positive, encouraging atmosphere and show my gratitude for their care.

I gazed at the wall before me, which was covered in a collage of pictures that highlighted the stark contrast between my current reality and the warmth of my past. Each photo depicted moments of joy and intimacy with my child, making the cold, clinical environment of the ICU feel even more alien. I was tormented by the thought of my baby being alone, deprived of her mother's comforting presence, and I was consumed with worry about how this separation might affect her growth and development.

My lips trembled and tears pooled in my eyes as I reached out and pointed to the pictures on the wall, trying to convey to Rachel why my heart was breaking. I missed my child with a depth that words could not fully capture. The emotional weight of being in the ICU, isolated from her, was nearly unbearable. My only longing was to hold her close, to feel her tiny body against mine, and to offer her the reassurance and love she so desperately needed.

I glanced up at the clock – 6:15. The shift change was imminent. I was alone in my room, a sense of solitude washing over me as I wondered where everyone had gone. The curtain was drawn shut, creating a cocoon of privacy. I turned my gaze to the right and saw the sun beginning to fade, casting a dim light over the top of the building. The constant beeping and whirring of machines formed a persistent backdrop to my thoughts.

I reached down to find my call button, which has become entangled beneath the sheets and tubes. Using my only functional arm, my left, I carefully maneuvered the sheet away and grasped the button. I pressed it firmly. Within a minute, Rachel reappeared, stepping back into the room.

D-A-L-E, I typed in desperation. I needed him to find out who my next nurse would be.

"He's outside making a phone call. I'll tell him you're awake when he comes back in."

T-H-A-N-K Y-O-U, I typed.

"Of course," she smiled and then left.

I was fixated on the shift change. Who would be next? Would they understand me and my needs? The same worries day in and day out – the schedule always caused me fear. I was terrified I would die under the next person's care.

They were responsible for keeping me alive and ensuring that these machines worked correctly. The thought that something could go wrong with the machines and they wouldn't be able to revive me was so scary. What if my machine started beeping and they couldn't respond in time? The fear of dying alone in this sterile room was paralyzing. If I didn't call for help, I might face the ultimate risk – my own death.

My mind was consumed by relentless, dark thoughts of mortality. I was overwhelmed by a wave of fear and helplessness, each moment amplifying my anxiety. My body was overcome by a cold, gripping terror that I couldn't control. My child needed me, and the desperation to stay alive felt like a battle against an invisible enemy. "Fight, Vanessa, fight. Don't give up," I chanted to myself, clinging to every ounce of strength and hope I could muster.

This couldn't be the end for someone who has always been vibrant and full of life, someone who had always stayed active and healthy. I glanced at the clock, which read 6:55 p.m., signaling in my head that my new nurse was about to start her shift. I also realized that the evening shift change meant that Dale had to head home, not because his help was no longer needed but because he, too, needed to get some rest.

Gripping his little wire-bound notebook, he walked out of the room. I couldn't move, so I couldn't see where he was going. I sat in my room all alone, heat waves rushing over me. The cool fan continued to blow on me, but it was not enough. My pillow roll fell, and my head fell with it.

Soon, Dale walked back into the room and saw that my head had fallen to the right. My eye gaze looked right. I was helpless, and I couldn't lift my head. He noticed my head drooping and came to adjust it. He grabbed a towel, rolled it up, and tucked it gently under the side of my head to keep it in alignment with the rest of my body.

He looked at me and said, "You're having nurse Andy. She's the same one you had last night." Thank you, God. I was so relieved to have the same great nurse on repeat and felt like I had drawn a winning lottery ticket.

Another Long Night

I was still feeling hot, but a rush of relief soared through my body. I knew I would survive another night with her around. I gave him a thumbs up which, at this point, was all the communication I could handle. Using the alphabet board simply took too much time and energy.

I stared at the wall in front of me, where dozens of 8 x 11 printouts of my daughter were displayed. Tears streamed down my face as the ache of missing her overwhelmed me. Dale noticed my rising sadness, walked over to my bed, and gently kissed the top of my head. The gesture brought bittersweet comfort, but my anxiety spiked as I realized what was coming. He had to leave.

The one person who understood my needs better than anyone else was about to go. Dale explained that he needed to head home but reassured me that the nurses had his number in case anything urgent arose.

"I'll see you in the morning," he said, but a wave of uncertainty gripped me. Would I really see him again? With Jared gone, too, I feared that this might be the end. The thought that I might never see him – or anyone else who understood my needs – again was overwhelming.

I watched with a heavy heart as Dale pulled the curtain aside, his silhouette briefly illuminated by the dim light before he stepped out of the room. The quiet of the empty room pressed in on me as I collapsed into tears. The sun had set long ago and darkness had settled over the room, casting shadows that obscured the images of my daughter on the wall. The only sounds were the soft, rhythmic beeping of the machines and my own muffled sobs. Suddenly, I heard the rustle of the curtain being pulled back once more and Andy stepped into the room, bringing a faint glimmer of hope into my world again.

"Hey," she said enthusiastically. "I'm glad to see you again. I hear you have communication papers now – that's great!" I tried to match her enthusiasm, but the fear and depression were just too intense. I ditched my communication papers and gave her a thumbs-up sign instead, and closed my eyes in hopes of making it all disappear.

She moved to my left side with a comforting presence, unscrewing the cap from my IV and gently inserting a mixture of medications which now included melatonin in an attempt to wean me from the stronger sleep medications.

"This should help you unwind and get some rest," she said softly, her voice filled with kindness as she offered a sense of calm in the midst of my anxiety. She made sure I had my call button nearby and gently tucked in my communication papers under the pile of plastic tubing on my lap before leaving my room.

I drifted off to sleep, only to be jolted awake at midnight. Panic set in as I lied in the darkness of the room. I glanced to my right and saw the city lights glowing brightly in the distance. My heart raced as I fumbled for my call button, pressing it urgently. Andy arrived quickly. I flipped to the front page of my communication papers and typed slowly: N-E-E-D S-L-E-E-P M-E-D-I-C-I-N-E.

Andy responded, "OK, let me see about getting you some Benadryl." While I hoped it would be effective, I remained skeptical. She left and returned with the medication, administering it through my IV. Although fear still churned within me, I managed to fall back asleep, but only briefly. I was soon awakened by a respiratory therapist adjusting my ventilator settings. I appreciated his effort, knowing that he was just doing his job, but I was frustrated because I understood how crucial sleep was for me.

I lied motionless for another hour, consumed by fear and uncertainty about my future. Unable to endure the solitude any longer, I hit the call button once more, desperately requesting additional medication. Andy arrived and sympathetically explained that she couldn't provide more at this time because the medical team was slowly weaning me from the heavy sleep medications I had been receiving. Instead, she offered to give me melatonin, which although it didn't do much to help me sleep, I was grateful for a more natural approach to helping me fall asleep.

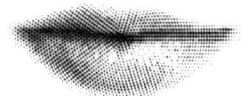

CHAPTER 5
Therapy Takes the Lead

I woke up unsure of the day and saw the sun beginning to rise over the buildings in the distance. I lied there, isolated and exhausted from a sleepless night, until someone entered the room. I wondered how the day would unfold and who my new nurse would be.

Andy stepped in and greeted me with a cheerful, "Good morning! How are you?" I slowly typed out T-I-R-E-D and then N-O S-L-E-E-P. She nodded in understanding, offering a comforting response, "Yeah, I know."

As the noises of the ICU grew louder with each passing minute, I wondered where Dale was. I desperately needed his presence to feel at ease.

I glanced at the clock as the hands approached 8 a.m. Rachel walked in, dressed in her familiar blue scrubs and wearing a reassuring I've-got-you-covered expression. Her presence was a tremendous relief; seeing her face again felt like a small comfort in this overwhelming situation.

The sound of footsteps grew louder as the curtains were drawn back, and Dale entered the room with Jared by his side. They came to my bedside and asked how my night was. I typed in reply, explaining my difficulty in staying asleep. Jared, trying to understand my emotional state, began asking questions.

My hands trembled as I spelled out, letter by letter, how terrified I had been. M-A-C-H-I-N-E-S, N-O-I-S-E, I typed with shaking fingers.

The anxiety was palpable as I continued. I was on life support machines. What would happen if they stopped working? The fear gripped me so tightly that it felt like I could barely breathe, my heart pounding in my chest. I imagined the ventilator malfunctioning, the alarms blaring, and no one getting to me in time.

The thought of dying alone in this sterile room, without seeing my daughter or saying goodbye, overwhelmed me. Jared's face showed concern, but he struggled to follow my slow, painstaking typing. Frustration set in for both of us, and for me, it mingled with fear. I fought to stay calm, determined to make them understand the depth of my terror. I slowed down and started again, hoping to convey my fears clearly to both of them.

Jared looked at me with a look of heartfelt compassion. "Vanessa, I understand your concerns, but this place is like Fort Knox. If anything goes wrong with any machine, we will be notified immediately." His reassuring tone offered a small comfort, but the anxiety still lingered. "If it would help you at all, I can take you across the hall to look at the telemetry room. Inside that room, there is a staff member, and their entire job is to monitor the functioning of each patient's equipment." His vivid description of what the telemetry room consisted of offered me a level of comfort I hadn't felt in some time.

The profound impact of his honesty, open communication, and face-to-face dialogue cannot be overstated. His offer to personally escort me to the room and alleviate my anxieties through direct reassurance was far more effective than any medication could have been. This approach was deeply impactful and highlights an important lesson for medical professionals: addressing anxiety with empathy and transparency can be a far more powerful and natural method than relying solely on medication.

Morning rounds resumed like clockwork. The group seemed

larger than the day before, but then again, I couldn't rotate my body to get a good glimpse of everyone there. The clock read 9:15.

Within a few minutes, the group in crisp white jackets started to disperse. However, a few familiar faces stuck around, talking and glancing in my direction. My heart raced, wondering what they were discussing. Why couldn't they come inside my room to talk to me? Were they preparing to tell me I was dying? I had no idea.

My paranoia got the best of me. They began to walk toward my room, pulling back the sliding door and curtain. I heard the neurologist say, "Hi, Vanessa." He went through his typical list of questions, as he did each morning. He asked me to follow his fingers and tracked the movement of my pupils. His body a few feet from mine, he asked me to squeeze his fingers.

I tried to comply, my muscles trembling with the effort. He listened to my chest with his stethoscope, the cold metal sending shivers through me. The neurologist discussed my condition in a calm, measured tone, but my mind raced with fear and uncertainty. What were they thinking? How much longer would I be trapped in this nightmare?

As he spoke, the rest of the team nodded, taking notes and exchanging glances. Dale sat back silently, taking notes on his own notepad. My anxiety spiked with each passing moment, my heart racing.

"The team is going to start physical therapy, occupational therapy, and speech therapy," he said. Thoughts swirled in my mind like a tornado out in the open desert. As a speech-language pathologist or SLP, I knew what PT, OT, and speech therapy meant all too well. I looked down at my lap, covered with sheets and plastic tubing.

Sprinting to Ventilator Freedom

"Your respiratory therapist is going to start sprinting you as well," the neurologist proceeded to say. I didn't know what sprinting was and felt so lost. There was so much I didn't know.

I looked down at my communication papers, a whole laundry list of questions flooding my mind. I noticed my fingers were trembling with nervousness as I inched them toward the papers. I squeezed them together, hoping to hide my nervousness.

The term "sprinting" had me concerned, so I typed, W-H-A-T I-S S-P-R-I-N-T-I-N-G, pointing slowly to one letter at a time.

Noticing my anxiety, Jared approached my bedside, making reassuring eye contact. His voice was calm and gentle as he spoke. "It's OK," he said softly, placing a comforting hand on my shoulder. "I know this is overwhelming, but we're here to help you through it."

He took a deep breath and continued, "You're on a ventilator right now, and it's doing all the work for your breathing. Sprinting is a process where we gradually help you spend more time breathing on your own, weaning you off the ventilator. We'll start by taking you off for short periods to see how you do without it. During these times, the team will be right here beside you, making sure you're alright."

His words were carefully chosen, each one intended to ease my fears. "We'll gradually increase the time you spend breathing on your own," he explained, "and we'll monitor you closely the entire time. It's a step-by-step process, and we'll go at your pace. You won't be alone. We'll be right here with you every step of the way, ensuring that you're safe and comfortable."

Jared's confidence and calm demeanor soothed my nerves. I nodded, trying to absorb the information and reassurance he was offering. "We'll take it one step at a time," he repeated, his eyes locked onto mine, "and we'll be right here with you."

"The team will be right here with you" resonated in my head and heart. I trusted him.

I felt a small sense of relief, but the fear of failure loomed large. W-H-A-T H-A-P-P-E-N-S I-F I C-A-N-'-T D-O T-H-I-S, I typed next, my fingers still trembling.

They all followed my fingers as I touched each letter on the board to ask my questions. It took so long, and I became anxious that they wouldn't be able to understand my worries.

Jared read my question and responded with compassion. "Vanessa, we understand this is hard. If you can't do it, we will keep trying. Your body changes every day, and we will adjust our approach as needed. We are here to help you through this. Focus on your daughter."

He was right. But I couldn't release the worry of the unknown. How did I get here? This wasn't my life. Look at your wall, look at your girl, I'd remind myself – she needs you. I no longer heard what the doctors were talking about and hoped Dale was listening for me.

I looked forward, right through them, at the wall behind them, covered in beautiful pictures of my innocent daughter who needed her mom back.

The neurologist continued, discussing a treatment protocol called plasmapheresis. This therapy, also called plasma exchange therapy and representing a range of procedures, in my case would be used to filter my blood for harmful antibodies that seemed to be attacking my nerves, before the blood was returned to my body. "We want to do four rounds of this treatment with you. We really don't know what the outcomes will be or if it will even work for you, but we need to start it soon."

I gave the team of white coats a fist symbol to show that I was prepared for the fight and willing to go through with whatever protocol they suggested, even if the outcome was uncertain. What did I have to lose? I didn't want to be that patient they talked about behind closed doors, saying that I gave up or wasn't motivated to get well. That wasn't me.

They all left, except Jared and Dale. Jared stayed. Why? I didn't know, but I was glad he did. With shaking fingers, I looked at him and started to type. Tears flowed down my face once again. Getting frustrated, I kept going. Now, I was lifeless in this hospital bed, attached to machines by countless tubes. In a complete state of overwhelm, I typed slowly, W-H-A-T H-A-P-P-E-N-E-D T-O M-E-?

Dale and Jared looked at each other, blank and sad looks upon each of their faces as if delivering bad news. "We really don't know, Vanessa. We're still trying to figure that out. I am sorry we don't have better news for you, but we do have a plan for now. I will be back to check on you later." Jared told Dale to page him if needed and left us both alone in the room to reflect on all the latest news.

My Floppy Right Arm

The curtain swished open once more, and a young woman stepped into the room. She was petite, probably in her mid-20s and with sandy blonde hair. As she approached my bed, she introduced herself as Stacy, my occupational therapist. I watched her with a mix of frustration and despair as she began outlining her plan for my care. My hands gripped my communication papers tightly, and the urge to tell her to leave me alone was overwhelming. But deep down, I knew she was there to help me, to assist in my recovery so I could return to my daughter. Be nice, I reminded myself.

Despite my inner turmoil, I was relieved that Rachel was still by my side. She seemed to sense my distress and provided silent support, understanding my needs even when I couldn't express them. But the day continued to spiral downward. First, I had faced speech therapy, and now I needed to begin occupational therapy. This wasn't the life I had imagined for myself, and the weight of it all was almost too much to bear.

She lowered my bed until I was lying flat and began explaining the plan: to get me to use my right arm from a side-lying position. Speechless, I stared at her with a look that surely conveyed my disbelief and frustration. "You're out of your mind if you think this arm is moving," I wanted to say, but forced myself to remain polite.

I tried to move my arm as directed, but it just flopped uselessly to the side like a lump of Jello. In a final, desperate attempt to show her the futility of the exercise, I used my left arm to lift the right one. It fell onto my head like rain, further emphasizing its lack of control.

Tears streamed down my face as I felt a wave of humiliation and anger. The simple task of moving my arm was beyond my capabilities, and the frustration was overwhelming. In a burst of frustration, I used my functioning arm to violently throw my communication papers and her clipboard onto the floor.

Dale walked in just as the clipboard hit the floor, his expression a mix of surprise and concern. He picked up the clipboard and handed it back to the occupational therapist without saying a word. I felt a flush of embarrassment; how could I explain or justify throwing someone's belongings when I couldn't speak and my communication papers were now on the floor? I was acutely aware of my behavior and wanted to convey my frustration, but now I regretted my behavior.

Surrounded by tubes, I managed to shift back to a flat position with the help of the nursing team. Before the occupational therapist left, I typed, T-H-A-N-K Y-O-U using my communication papers, desperate to show my appreciation and maintain some semblance of politeness. I knew that despite my anger and frustration, I needed her help far more than she needed me.

Battered and Bruised Veins

I grabbed my papers and touched the neck picture symbol, indicating to Dale that I needed an adjustment. He loosened up the towel rolls on the side of my head and tucked them back in.

Through the bars on the window, I could see that the sun was beginning to set, signaling the end of another exhausting day. The hallways were slowly calming down, with noticeably less foot traffic coming in and out of my room. I braced myself for the arrival of my night nurse when Jared walked in.

A mix of fear and relief swept through me – fear of what he might say about my prognosis and relief in knowing there was someone who genuinely cared, someone who was devoted and would help us.

Despite my exhaustion and lack of desire for small talk, I was anxious to hear what he had to say. Jared, though young, was incredibly knowledgeable and intelligent. I felt a surge of gratitude for his presence, knowing he was there to support both Dale and me. I gripped my communication papers, anticipating the questions he would ask.

Jared exchanged a glance with Dale before looking back at me. My eyes darted right, then left, filled with apprehension about the news he was about to share. Would it be bleak, or worse, terminal? My hands shook as I held my papers nervously. I typed, W-H-A-T-'-S N-E-X-T-? I-'-M S-C-A-R-E-D. As I pointed to the pictures plastered on the wall ahead of me, tears ran down my face. I needed them to know I missed my baby and needed to get home to her.

Jared and Dale looked at the wall, then back at each other. Jared spoke first, his voice quiet and the moment thick with tension.

"They are going to start your first round of plasmapheresis sometime tonight. Your nurse is going to help us locate veins that will hold up for the treatment. I'll be back tomorrow morning to ensure that everything is going OK, but in the meantime, I hope you can rest, knowing you are safe here and receiving the best care." He gave me a list of meditations to listen to as well as affirmations to recite in my head, then he left the room.

Glancing over the affirmations and hearing him say those words, I felt a mix of relief and anxiety. The thought of more needles and procedures was daunting, but his reassurances provided some comfort. I knew in my heart that UCSD was the best place for me to get the answers and care I needed. As he spoke, I clung to his words, hoping to draw strength from his calm demeanor.

I fully agreed with him. In my heart, I knew without a doubt that being at a teaching hospital like this was the best place for us to get answers. Despite the fear and uncertainty swirling inside me, a small flicker of hope remained. I was surrounded by a team which genuinely cared for us both, and that meant everything. Tears welled up in my eyes, a mixture of relief and overwhelming gratitude.

In the midst of this nightmare, I found solace in knowing I was in the right place, fighting with the best possible support. As he left, Dale looked at me, adjusted my head and towel rolls one last time, kissed my forehead and said his goodbye as well.

Wishing they would stay around to offer their presence and comfort during the first of four treatments, I felt a pang of loneliness. The thought of facing this alone and with the possibility of training a new nurse was terrifying. However, I knew they both needed to go home. As the reality of their departures sank in, the fear of being left to face this daunting battle alone overwhelmed me. This was my battle to face, but the weight of their absence made the upcoming treatment feel even more daunting.

Minutes after Dale left, a new and unfamiliar woman in scrubs entered my room. Getting used to the routine, I assumed she was my new nurse. Panic surged through me, knowing she was new and unfamiliar with my care. The realization that she would be responsible for inserting new IV lines into my worn and depleted veins heightened my anxiety.

She was tall and beautiful, with long, blonde hair flowing as if she had just left a hair salon. Her makeup was done tastefully, and she exuded positivity and patience. I glanced at her badge, which read, "Laura." She saw me crying and immediately grabbed a tissue. She looked up at the wall and smiled.

"Is that your daughter?" she asked. I gave her a thumbs up, feeling embarrassed that this was the first time she was meeting me, but I couldn't hold back the tears.

"What's her name?" she asked. I typed her name.

"She's beautiful. I bet you miss her. We're going to get you out of here, OK?"

I cried more. I wanted to hug Laura and thank her for her kindness, but I couldn't move. I couldn't stop crying as I ached for my daughter. Laura changed the subject, likely in an attempt to curb my uncontrolled emotions. Her calm and reassuring tone helped me refocus my attention and gain back some of my fighting spirit. I couldn't help but think how much influence the nurse's attitude and disposition had on a patient's willingness and perseverance through the darkest of times.

The condition of my veins was dire. They were bruised and scarred from countless needle sticks over the past two weeks. The once-pristine paths for IV access were now a battleground of dark purple and red, resembling a topographical map of trauma. The skin was taut and tender, and each vein felt fragile, as if a gentle touch might cause them to collapse. The challenge of finding a viable vein was daunting, and the thought of another attempt only intensified my dread.

Laura was cautious and precise, fully aware of how critical this procedure was for me. Each attempt to find a usable vein was successful, and with each successful insertion into my skin, I felt a profound wave of relief wash over me. I exhaled deeply, knowing that the most crucial part of the procedure had been accomplished and that I could now focus on the next steps of my recovery.

Immediately afterward, a short woman with long, flowing black hair and large glasses with black frames appeared at my bedside. She was pushing a large machine, about the height of her own body, on a cart. It was white with sleek, silver surfaces reflecting the harsh fluorescent lights of the room. Various tubes snaked out from the machine, coiling like serpents, ready to connect to my already bruised and battered veins.

Small monitors displayed information that I could not see. All I heard was the beeping and low, quiet hum of the machine next to me. She introduced herself as the woman who would administer my plasmapheresis treatments. Exhausted and too tired for another typing experience, I gave her a thumbs up. She looked at both arms, inspecting the IV lines Laura had strategically placed in them, and got to work.

Her presence brought a mix of relief and anxiety. While I was grateful that the treatment was starting, I couldn't shake the worry of wondering whether this would even work. As she prepared the machine, the room felt warmer and more sterile.

The reality of the treatment set in, and I braced myself for the next step in this battle. She unscrewed the caps on my IV and carefully inserted the tubes from the machine. Within minutes, the machine slowly began to feed the new medication into my body.

I watched as the liquid plasma moved through the tubes, feeling a chill run down my spine. Each drop represented hope mingled with uncertainty. My body tensed as I shifted my arms around with discomfort. The machine beeped. "I need you to stay as still as possible," the woman said gently. "This machine is very sensitive, and if you move too often, it stops working."

That was it – the start of the plasmapheresis treatment. My veins, already battered and bruised, reluctantly accepted the medication, and I could only hope it would make a difference. Exhaustion overtook me and I drifted off to sleep. It was nearly midnight when she completed the procedure.

I had slept intermittently throughout the night, with constant interruptions from the respiratory therapist and the relentless shuffle of the 24-hour nursing staff around the ICU. Laura, recognizing my frustration with the noise, thoughtfully placed a sign outside my door asking for quiet in an attempt to aid in my sleep and healing. In a tender gesture of care, she gently applied lavender essential oils to my feet.

The warm, soothing sensation of the lavender gliding over my skin was calming and melted away some of my anxiety. As the soothing scent filled the room, I felt a wave of relaxation wash over me, providing a brief respite from the stress and helping me find a moment of peace amidst the chaos.

A new day had begun, and I woke up after yet another restless night full of anxiety over the new plan. The noise in my room increased as the shift change rolled through the ICU. I hit my call button in the usual panic to find out who my next nurse was. I fumbled around with my fingertips, searching for my communication papers. I found them buried under my sheet and, using my left arm, pulled them out from under the covers.

Laura entered my room. I grabbed my communication papers and started to type, W-H-O I-S M-Y D-A-Y N---. She cut me off and asked, "Do you want to know who your day nurse is?"

Y-E-S, I typed.

You're going to have a new nurse today." Knowing I struggled with nurse anxiety, she quickly tried to soothe my fears. She walked over to my bedside, took my hand, and looked me in the eyes. "Vanessa, you're a fighter," she said. "You can do this. You are so strong. Just keep your focus on your daughter, okay? Your nurse today is Cat. She's really great. I've reviewed all your needs with her and shared everything she needs to know to take care of you. You truly are in good hands."

I stared blankly at her, tears streaming down my face, hoping to convey how scared I was of a new person caring for me and my uncertainty about what I needed to feel comfortable. She squeezed my hands, indicating that she was about to leave. I silently pleaded with her not to go, but I knew there was no use. I understood she had to leave, and I had to surrender to the idea of having a new nurse.

Feeling so depleted and exhausted, but eternally grateful for her sensitivity, I could feel her compassion for her job and her patience running so deep within her. As she walked out the door to go home, the usual hot flash of anxiety flooded my body.

As I kicked off the sheets, I turned my gaze to the door just as Cat walked in, dressed in blue scrubs. She was short, with dark almond-shaped eyes and long, flowing brown hair pulled back from her face. She approached my bedside, glanced up at the pictures on the wall, and then looked back at me, lying motionless and covered in tubes in my bed.

"Hey, Vanessa," she said with a warm smile as she looked at me. Curious about the pictures, she asked if that was my daughter. Y-E-S, I typed, tears streaming down my face, hoping she would understand that I was a mom wanting to be home with my precious girl. She gently pushed the tubes aside, took my hand, looked me in the eye, and pointed to the wall, saying, "She needs you." I knew she was right, and I appreciated her taking the time to understand who I was and what I needed in that moment. I was not just a number; I was a mother, and I could sense that she understood that. I didn't know this woman, but I felt a connection.

As I absorbed her words, a sense of calm began to wash over me. The weight of my fears lightened just a bit, and for the first time in a while, I felt a flicker of hope. I could envision my daughter's smile, and it gave me strength to face the challenges ahead.

She shifted the topic. "You have a busy day ahead—physical therapy will begin today," she said. Just then, Dale walked into the room. He glanced over at Cat, introduced himself, and then came straight to my bedside, gently touching my leg.

"How did you sleep and how did the treatment go?" he asked, hoping for positive news.

Getting frustrated with the slowness of communicating I typed, O-K, then L-O-N-G followed by T-I-R-E-D. I started to omit less important words to save time.

"What time did they finish your treatment?" he asked.

L-A-T-E. V-E-I-N-S H-E-L-D U-P, I typed, followed by a thumbs up indicating some positive news.

A Very Scary Discussion About Extubation

Dale turned and looked over his shoulder as the crowd of white jackets gathered outside my room. It was time for morning rounds. He looked at Cat and pointed to the door, indicating he was going to step out and see what the team had to say. She followed right behind him, leaving me alone in the room. I pulled my call button near, just in case. The large group dispersed and like clockwork, a smaller group entered my room and assembled at the foot of my bed, with Jared among them.

The team leader began a very matter-of-fact discussion with, "We have placed orders to do another MRI on your brain, Vanessa, so expect that to happen sometime soon. Physical therapy will be in today as well. The team will also continue to work on sprinting with you. The goal is to get you going for longer periods of time without the ventilator. We need to see if you can breathe without it," the doctor said, his voice tinged with an undertone of seriousness. "We're planning to try extubating you soon."

The mention of extubation sent a jolt of anxiety through me and scared me to my core.

The doctor continued, his words now more detailed as if trying to provide some clarity amidst my mounting fear. "Extubation involves carefully removing the breathing tube that's been supporting your breathing. We'll do this by slowly removing the tube while ensuring you're able to breathe on your own."

As he spoke, he described the process in greater detail. "We'll first make sure you're in stable condition. You'll be closely monitored for any signs of distress or difficulty breathing. If you can breathe adequately on your own, we'll continue to observe and support you as needed. If not, we may need to re-intubate you and consider other options, like placing a tracheostomy, to ensure your airway remains open and functional."

My heart pounded in my chest as I envisioned the procedure. The thought of having the tube removed, with its associated risks and uncertainties, was overwhelming. I imagined the team working around me – nurses and doctors, all focused on ensuring that the procedure went smoothly.

The doctor's words were punctuated by technical terms and procedural details, but my mind was clouded by fear. I could feel the sweat increasing, and I kicked off the sheets in an attempt to find some relief. The prospect of potentially not being able to breathe on my own filled me with dread, and my eyes were fixed on the wall, my longing to be with my daughter intensifying with every passing moment.

The extubation procedure, while crucial for my recovery, felt like an insurmountable hurdle. The reality of the situation weighed heavily on me, and I hoped that Dale, who was always meticulous about taking notes, was capturing every detail, even as I struggled to absorb the information myself. They left the room, leaving Dale and Jared alone with me and my thoughts. I looked them in the eyes, gripped my communication papers, and typed out my daughter's name, hoping these two men would understand the enormity of all that was just conveyed to me and the fearful uncertainty I felt about whether I could ever be the mother I wanted to be again.

I kicked the sheets signaling I was hot. Jared gently pulled the sheets off my legs, revealing my dingy yellow socks. I stared blankly at my daughter's face on the wall in front of me, my mind drifting further away from their world.

In sadness, I told myself that they didn't get it. They were so kind and I didn't want to hurt their feelings, but they just didn't get it. I had to focus on my daughter and yet was grieving all the losses I had experienced in the past few weeks. I pointed at the wall in front of me. I pointed at my daughter.

My eyes met Jared's, and I pointed again. I wanted him to see what mattered to me, what would get me through this. What he said didn't matter to me, I just wanted it all to end and was willing to do whatever they needed me to do to get there. Around noon, Cat left for her lunch break and a replacement nurse was called in. I was left wondering if she would be present for the extubation that I knew was on the immediate horizon.

Extubation

My room soon filled up; my team of doctors had arrived for the process of removing the breathing tube. Jared stood next to Dale, offering unwavering support to both of us. I felt fortunate that he was my doctor and deeply appreciated his steady presence during every difficult procedure and conversation.

Another unexpected face in the room was my social worker, Tracy. Whether she had been called in specifically or just happened to be there, I couldn't say, but she stood with the rest, waiting for the procedure to begin.

The doctors gathered at the foot of my bed, explaining the extubation procedure. They told me I would need to cough as they pulled the tube out and that they would then monitor how I responded. What I didn't know then was that the anesthesiologist wasn't responding to pages. They needed his presence in case things went south and his absence forced the team to call a code blue, indicating a critical patient status.

Cat, just about to take a bite of her lunch, heard the call from the cafeteria and immediately knew it was for me. She rushed back to my bedside, realizing the urgency. She was then sent back to lunch as it wasn't as urgent as expected; the anesthesiologist had responded to the call after all.

With all eyes on me, I felt terrified. The procedure could either go well, allowing me to breathe on my own and bringing me closer to going home, or it could go very wrong, leading to a tracheostomy. My mind raced with panic. What if my lungs couldn't handle it? What if my throat closed up and I couldn't get enough air?

The thought of another invasive procedure, another tube, another obstacle, loomed over me. I feared the pain, the uncertainty, and the possibility of something going wrong. The weight of these fears pressed down on me, making it hard to focus on the hopeful outcome everyone else seemed to be counting on.

On the count of three, the nurse pulled the tube out as I coughed. Thick mucus spewed from my mouth, a clear liquid that seemed to flow endlessly. As I tried to take my first breath, my vocal cords malfunctioned, closing off my airway.

I produced a horrible gasping sound.

My chest tightened as I struggled for air, each second feeling like forever. My heart pounded, and fear gripped me tighter with every failed attempt to breathe.

One doctor, his face etched with worry, fixated on my inability to properly breathe, and he immediately approached the side of my bed holding something in his hand. He placed it on my neck, but I couldn't focus on what it was. He listened intently.

My eyes felt like they were going to pop out of my head. I looked up at the pictures of my daughter on the wall, thinking, "This is it. I'm dying." I was so scared, gripping the sides of the bed rail.

I looked at my daughter's pictures, thinking this was the last time I would see her. I wouldn't have the opportunity to properly say goodbye, tell her how proud I was of her, and kiss her one last time. My heart raced as I struggled for air, each second stretching into what felt like an eternity.

Every breath was a battle, and I felt like I was losing.

Jared jumped into a protective mode. He looked over at Dale and instructed him to leave the room, not wanting him to witness what was unfolding as I gasped for air. Dale clung to the bed, his eyes wide with fear and desperation, and he refused to leave my side.

Tracy and Jared acted quickly, knowing there wasn't much time. They pried his fingers off my bed rail and dragged his heavy body out of the room as he struggled, an immense look of worry across his face. They sat him down and closed the door behind him, cutting off all sound to my room.

Everything went black, and life ended as I knew it.

When I woke up, I couldn't move. The sensation of nakedness overcame me, though I knew I must have been covered. Nurses were wiping my legs with a wet towel. Slowly, I began to wiggle my toes, my only way to signal that I was still alive. "You're OK, Vanessa," the nurses reassured me, touching my feet as I wiggled my toes – my silent plea for acknowledgment.

As I regained awareness, it became clear that I had failed the extubation. I was overwhelmed with anger, sadness, and embarrassment. This failure meant I was not leaving the ICU anytime soon; instead, I would need a tracheostomy.

Tracheostomy

The following morning was the day of the tracheostomy surgery. My anxiety was somewhat alleviated when I saw that Cat was my nurse again. She had been a very comforting presence. Aware of what was happening today, Lindsey, my speech pathologist, came into my room with 'Trache Tom,' a plastic model of the human airway, to explain the procedure. She used it as a visual aid to help me understand how my airflow would be redirected through the tracheostomy and how I would eventually be able to vocalize again.

She patiently walked me through each step, answering questions and ensuring that I felt as prepared as possible. My anxiety crept up again as each word left her mouth, with every detail of the surgery causing my body temperature to rise. The thought of producing a possibly permanent hole in my neck and inserting a tube to help me breathe was terrifying.

Being so aware of the procedure had its challenges; my mind was dizzy with fears of complications, infections, and the potential for lifetime dependency on the tracheostomy. I could feel my heart pounding and sense my palms sweating profusely.

Before the tracheostomy procedure, an Ear, Nose, Throat (ENT) consult had been ordered to assess the function of my vocal folds. The procedure required inserting a scope through my nose and down into my throat to examine my vocal folds. The ENT first applied lidocaine to numb my right nostril. As the endoscope was gently guided in, they found no evidence of suspicious masses, lesions, or ulcerations. The vocal folds were moving normally, closing and opening as expected. The only thing noted was an unusual amount of secretions pooling in the pyriform sinuses.

That procedure was the last thing I recall from before the surgery. They must have sedated me at this point because I didn't remember going in for surgery; everything in my memory had faded. One moment I was lying in my hospital bed, grappling with the tidal wave of anxiety, and the next, I was waking up post-surgery in my bed. The transition was a blur.

After the surgery, I woke up feeling groggy but relieved that it was over. The first thing I noticed was the absence of the uncomfortable endotracheal tube that had been lying on my lip for what seemed like ages. Cat was there, her calm presence reassuring me as she checked the new tracheostomy site. She explained that everything had gone smoothly and that the tube was functioning as expected.

Members of my team were pleasantly shocked as they walked into my room. They had become so accustomed to seeing me with a tube in my mouth, obscuring my face. Now, for what felt like the first time, they finally got to see the real me behind all the tubes.

Their eyes widened with surprise and joy, and I could sense their relief and happiness. It was a moment of triumph, a small but significant step toward reclaiming my identity and moving forward on the road to wellness. The surgery marked a significant turning point in my recovery.

Now all I needed to do was wean off the ventilator so I could leave the ICU setting and get back to my life. However, before anything else, I needed to survive.

Realizing that the surgery was over, the tracheostomy was in place, and it was time to embark on a new phase terrified me. The enormity of the situation hit me hard, leaving me feeling profoundly alone and overwhelmed. I was also uncertain about what the future would bring now with the tracheostomy. The feelings of overwhelm were too great, and the uncertainty of adapting to this new reality was daunting. The weight of the unknown made the journey forward seem even more challenging, amplifying my fear and isolation.

In those moments of intense fear, I had to constantly remind myself that I had a good team supporting me. Even though I was unable to talk, I still had Dale by my side, providing unwavering support and reassurance. His presence was a crucial comfort, helping to alleviate some of the fear and uncertainty that accompanied this new phase of my medical journey.

Over the next few days, my care team worked diligently to help me adapt to the tracheostomy. I had difficulties breathing and required frequent suctioning, so I was constantly pressing the call button, requesting help. The chronic suctioning caused significant concern about infection, but I wasn't sure what else to do. My respiratory system was too weak to cough up all the secretions my body was spontaneously producing.

The sensation of trying to clear my airway was both exhausting and distressing. Every attempt to cough up the thick, sticky secretions felt like a battle. The nature of my neck paralysis certainly didn't make the act any easier. The mucus clung stubbornly to my throat, making each breath feel labored and obstructed. My chest and abdominals ached from the strain, and my neck ached with every effort to expel the mucus.

Just when I had felt things were getting better, this felt like a tremendous setback. The constant need for assistance and the looming threat of infection weighed heavily on my mind. Each cough drained my energy, leaving me feeling more depleted. The relentless cycle of suctioning and coughing made me question my progress and whether I would ever regain a sense of normalcy and be the mom I wanted to be again.

How Many Physical Therapists Does It Take?

A young girl with golden brown hair pulled back into a ponytail approached my bedside. Looking over at her badge, I saw the letters PT. She looked at Dale and shook hands with him, introducing herself as Jess. I couldn't help but notice that Jess had a smile that lit up the room.

She looked at me and asked how I was feeling. I typed out word by word how tired I was from the late-night plasmapheresis treatment. Her facial expressions radiated empathy and genuine concern, and I immediately felt a connection to her. I felt safe.

She spoke with such optimism and fearlessness as she discussed my physical therapy goals for the day. I also couldn't help but feel scared—more accurately, terrified—at the idea of moving my body in any way. Every movement felt like a mountain to climb, and I was overwhelmed by the thought of pushing myself beyond what felt safe. But at the same time, I didn't want to be the patient who gave up or didn't at least try.

Therefore, I was in complete shock when she asked for backup to get me out of bed. She needed my nurse, respiratory therapist, and occupational therapist for additional support. She explained to Dale how the transfer would look, her voice betraying her acknowledgment of the challenge ahead.

Each member of the team gathered around, forming a semi-circle at the foot of my bed, their faces a mix of determination and concern. She strategically moved the tubes off my lap as best she could to allow my body some freedom to move. As she did this, she inadvertently moved my communication papers.

My lifeline of communication was out of reach and I panicked. The room seemed to close in around me as I struggled to cope with the sudden loss of control. Dale was nearby, so that offered some comfort as he could be my voice. I caught his eye, silently pleading for reassurance.

She raised the back of my bed to a 90-degree angle. My legs, thin and weak from disuse, were rotated over to the left side of the bed. My upper body, lacking the strength to support itself, slouched to the right, crumpled like a wet noodle. My right arm hung uselessly at my side, a heavy and unresponsive weight that added to my overall sense of helplessness. I felt a mixture of anxiety and determination, knowing that this simple movement was a monumental challenge for me now.

"On three," she instructed everyone, her voice tense with focus. "One, two, three," and the team lifted my body, pivoted it around and now had me sitting bedside. But they forgot my head. It fell forward, my neck unable to support the weight, and wouldn't stay erect.

Dale, can you get her head?" Jess immediately asked, worry in her voice. The urgency heightened my anxiety. Dale quickly moved to my side, placing one hand on each side of my head to hold it in place. His touch was careful, but my paralyzed neck muscles couldn't support it. I felt mortified as I sensed his gentle strength, realizing how vulnerable I was in that moment.

Jess, her voice calm but urgent, said she needed a neck brace before proceeding. She instructed the team to lay me back down. Exhausted, I was grateful to lie back down, hoping the next attempt would go smoother.

Dale, knowing how crucial my communication papers were for my sense of safety, handed them back to me. With shaky fingers, I pointed to the letters spelling out "neck pain." Rachel, always in tune with my needs, quickly responded, "OK, let me go get you some lidocaine patches."

She returned shortly, carrying the patches with a look of empathy. Gently, she placed them around my right neck and shoulders, her touch careful and soothing. The cool sensation of the patches brought relief, although not the heavy relief I received from prior doses of medications, but I knew they were trying to wean me off all heavy narcotics at this point.

Jess returned, now carrying a neck brace. The team resumed their duties, gently rotating my body out of the bed until I was in a sitting position. Dale gripped the sides of my head until the brace was in place, but it wasn't tight enough to support my neck, causing it to bobble back and forth. I felt a mix of anxiety and fear as they worked to stabilize me.

Frustration set in until Dale had an idea. He stuffed towels inside the brace, creating makeshift support. This worked, filling the gaps and holding my neck securely. It felt awkward and uncomfortable, and I quickly started hating the feeling of having to wear it, however it was necessary to ensure my safety while walking.

"Let's try to get her to stand on three," Jess instructed. Everyone bent over, gripping different parts of my body, their faces showing determination. As they prepared to lift me, a wave of fear washed over me. Rachel glanced at the heart rate monitor with concern but continued. "One, two, three." My body felt weak and unsteady, my legs trembling as I struggled to find balance. I managed to stand, but every muscle in my body quivered with exhaustion.

With the IV pole and ventilator at my side, I took a tentative step forward, each movement feeling as monumental as my daughter's first steps. The surreal nature of the experience struck me deeply. A nurse followed closely with a wheelchair, ready for a quick assist if needed. I felt larger than life, convinced that I was walking faster than I truly was and that I had covered a significant distance. But navigating the space while surrounded by IV tubes added to the challenge, making each step feel cumbersome and awkward. As my heart rate spiked beyond normal limits, the team decided I needed to rest. They helped me back to bed, and a wave of defeat and embarrassment washed over me when I realized I had only managed to walk six feet.

Jess looked at me with a smile and praised me for the great job I did. However, I didn't feel like I had accomplished anything spectacular. I wanted her to understand my previous abilities and hoped she wouldn't give up on me. I longed to share how physically active I once was, but the words wouldn't come. I stared blankly at her, hoping she would somehow grasp my feelings, even through that empty expression.

Everyone left the room except Dale, who stayed behind with a calm presence. I sat there, grieving my previous life and missing the familiarity of being home with my family. Tears flowed down my face, and an insurmountable fear flooded my body, leaving me feeling utterly lost in my uncertainty.

Dale, noticing I was feeling immense despair at my slow progress, created a list of daily accomplishments and posted it on the wall. It included the following:

- Completed plasmapheresis
- Finished my first OT session
- Used an AAC device
- Got out of bed and walked with PT
- Wore neck brace

This list was meant to show me that I was progressing and help me focus on any accomplishment I achieved during the day, no matter how small. Although many of these accomplishments felt minor and often meaningless, I focused on them as I reflected on the day and attempted to fall asleep, putting the events of the day behind me.

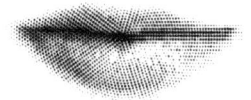

CHAPTER 6
Are Those Gunshots I'm Hearing in the MRI?

Nighttime Awakening

I was jolted awake hours later by a flurry of nursing staff. It was dark, and the only light came from a computer screensaver, casting shadows around my bed. "Vanessa, we need to take you for an MRI right now," Andy said with urgency.

My body tensed. I wanted to ask questions, and I remembered I had a way to communicate. Trembling with fear, I reached for my communication papers, my fingers moving quickly toward them.

Panicked, I typed frantically, N-O-! N-E-E-D D-A-L-E. C-A-L-L D-A-L-E. Andy watched me intently.

I begged her, shaking, tears running down my face. I N-E-E-D D-A-L-E-! C-A-L-L D-A-L-E-!-!

I couldn't do the MRI without Dale, and why were they whisking me away in the middle of the night? I was so scared but I forced myself to stay calm. The ventilator blared and the respiratory team rushed in to make adjustments. "Vanessa, we need you to remain calm," Andy said, her voice steady but urgent. "You're going to be OK. There isn't time to call Dale right now. We need to get this MRI done so the doctors can review your scans first thing in the morning. It has to happen now."

Frantically, with hands trembling, I typed, N-O-! I C-A-N-'-T-! C-A-L-L D-A-L-E N-O-W-!

"There's no time. You need to do this now," she said.

N-E-E-D M-E-D-S, I typed quickly, running out of time. I needed something to help me through this. H-O-W L-O-N-G W-I-L-L T-H-I-S T-A-K-E-? I typed.

"This one will take over an hour, Vanessa, and they need to get a full brain and spine MRI." The temperature in the room was spiking with each word I typed. "I will give you some medication to help you relax before you go in. Don't worry."

I stared at her tearfully as she squeezed my hand and said, "You can do this, Vanessa." She pointed toward the wall in front of me, and I quickly glanced at my daughter's beautiful face once more. The thought of her growing up without me was unbearable. Feeling cornered and with no other options, I looked at her and surrendered. The fear of bad results and the emotional weight of a terminal diagnosis weighed heavily on me. Andy administered a mixture of meds into my IV to calm me down, and through my tears, I drifted off into merciful sleep.

I was reawakened by bright lights and the sounds of voices walking past my bed in the Radiology Department. I wanted them to know I was scared and had concerns about being in there for an hour, but I couldn't tell them. My communication papers were gone.

A man in blue scrubs approached my bedside and explained the procedure. He tugged at the sheets under me and dragged my limp and deteriorating body from the already uncomfortable hospital bed onto an even more uncomfortable piece of hard plastic.

The fear of what this MRI would show got the best of me. My vision went black. All I could see was black, as dark as a nighttime sky without a single star. I couldn't see anything. "What's happening? Is this how it ends?" I asked myself bleakly.

As I felt them adjusting and tugging at my body, I was convinced I was dying and that no one knew it. I believed that all the symptoms with my vision were due to the progressive nature of the disease, but I later found out they were caused by the medication, not the illness itself.

"Vanessa, you're going to be OK," a man said. "We're going to put you in the machine, and it's very important that you stay as still as possible."

The more I cooperated, the faster this would be done, I thought to myself. That is, if I didn't die. If I did actually die, this would all end anyway.

"Vanessa, we're going to start now. If you need to come out for any reason, please press this button." They handed me something that felt like a remote control in my hand and put my finger on the button so I could feel it.

They didn't know that I couldn't see, and I couldn't tell them I needed more medication. I needed to be put to sleep to tolerate this. As my body slowly moved into the machine, I heard only the quiet hum of the MRI, but nothing from the outside.

Tap, tap, tap. Bang, bang. Suddenly sounds like gunfire erupted around me. I clutched the remote button they gave me, reminding myself to stay still. An hour to go and the fear was already overwhelming. The noise intensified, stretching into what felt like endless minutes of gunfire. I couldn't bear it any longer and pressed the remote button, desperate for relief.

"Vanessa, you're OK," a voice reassured me. "You can do this." He tried to comfort me, but he didn't grasp the depth of my fear. I felt like someone was shooting at me, that I was surrounded by phantom gunshots, and I couldn't communicate this terror.

"We really need to get this done tonight," he said, injecting more Ativan into my veins. The darkness turned into a swirling mix of colors, reminding me of the kaleidoscopes I played with as a child. It was beautiful, like a fireworks display.

But the beauty was overshadowed by the loud thumping and banging of the machine, which sounded like it was being hit with a hammer. The beeping grew louder, and the noises became like those of a construction site around me.

My mind raced. Was this real? Was I dying? The gunshot sounds intensified and seemed to confirm my worst fears. Maybe I was already dead, and this was what the afterlife felt like – a colorful, strange dream. It got quiet. I gave in to this thought and drifted off to sleep.

The noise started again and woke me up. I gripped the remote. Was I alive or dead? I pressed the button repeatedly, hoping someone would come. The bed shifted under me.

"Vanessa, you're doing OK. We only have about 20 minutes left," the man in scrubs reassured me. I wondered if this was what they said to people who had died. Maybe heaven is dark, but the kaleidoscope is its only light. The colors kept swirling until I fell asleep again.

Waking up the Next Morning

I woke up, unsure whether I was dreaming or was really back in my bed. Was this a dream or was I alive? My vision had returned and I looked at the pictures of my daughter on the wall. I must be alive, I decided.

I glanced to the right and saw the metal bars on the windows of the ICU. The clock showed 6:45, signaling the impending morning shift change. I moved my finger slowly to the call button and pressed it. Moments later, the nurse's voice came through the speaker, saying that she was on her way.

Andy pulled the curtain back and said, "Good morning, Vanessa." I couldn't help but wonder how she could be so energetic after the gunshot and kaleidoscope show from the night before. But I put that behind me. The communication papers were in front of me, buried under the tubes on my lap. With my left arm, I strategically moved the tubes and retrieved them. I began typing, W-H-O I-S M-Y D-A-Y N-U-R-S-E-? I touched each letter slowly so that she could decipher what I was saying.

"Rachel is back again today," she stated with a smile, knowing that would make me happy. I give her the thumbs up, feeling relieved. Andy looked at me and said, "Keep fighting and don't give up." As she pointed to the wall in front of me, I started crying, and she knew she was right. That little girl in the image on the wall in front of me needed me.

The ICU started coming alive for another day. The noise level picked up and the throng of beautiful, nicely dressed, white-coat professionals began inundating the rooms and halls.

The curtain pulled back and Dale arrived. Soon my entire team entered my small, cozy room. Everyone looked familiar at this point except one new woman. They all looked at each other and exchanged glances with Dale. There was an awkward silence as I waited for someone to speak. I was wondering whether they would discuss the events and results of the previous night's MRI. The new woman was likely in her 50s and introduced herself as Dr. G, a neurologist. I observed her closely – she seemed like a seasoned doctor with years of experience.

"Vanessa, can you tell me how many fingers I'm holding up?" she asked me. I held up one finger.

"How many clocks do you see?" she asked. Again, I held up one finger.

"Follow my fingers with one eye," she prompted me. "Great. Your vision appears to be back to normal," she stated. The white coats looked at each other but remained speechless and expressed little.

"Vanessa, we still don't have any answers as to what's going on at this point. We reviewed the scans from last night, and it doesn't appear that the brain lesions located on the medulla and pons are continuing to grow." This was the first time I had heard the terms "lesions" and "medulla and pons" together. I started to piece it all together, remembering back to grad school days and recalling that the medulla is crucial for regulating breathing, heart rate, and other vital functions, while the pons plays a key role in motor control and sensory analysis. Additionally, the pons works in conjunction with the medulla to control respiratory rhythm.

It slowly started to make sense. Understanding the involvement of these critical brain structures deepened my concern and highlighted the complexity of my condition.

"We're sorry we don't have more information for you, but we will continue to administer the last three rounds of plasmapheresis," my neurologist continued. "Again, we really don't know whether it will help. It's simply one of those things where you may feel different the next day or possibly a week or month later. We just don't know, but we'll keep trying."

I gave them all a fist pump, indicating that I would fight on and not give up and that they shouldn't give up on me either.

The room quieted as everyone left except for Dale and Dr. G, who stayed with me. Feeling some comfort in having another woman there, I slowly reached for my communication papers. I hoped, woman to woman, she might understand my deep longing to be with my child and my urgent need to leave this place.

Noticing my attempt to communicate, she moved closer to my bed and read what I was typing. My hands trembled as I typed, H-A-V-E Y-O-U S-E-E-N T-H-I-S B-E-F-O-R-E-? Each letter I typed, she repeated, ensuring that she understood. I looked her in the eyes, hoping she would understand the depths of my despair.

I returned to my communication papers, needing more details about two patients she had seen with my diagnosis. I typed slowly, H-O-W A-R-E T-H-E-Y N-O-W-?

"I'm sorry, I didn't get that. Can you repeat it?" she asked.

I forced myself to slow down. H-O-W A-R-E T-H-E-Y N-O-W-? I typed again, hoping I went slowly enough.

"One is doing OK and the other isn't doing well." I did the math – 50/50, not great odds. Tears welled up and I couldn't meet her eyes. What she was essentially saying was that I had a 50/50 chance of being the mom I'd always wanted to be. I couldn't accept this devastating news.

More questions flooded my mind. I typed, P-R-O-G-N-O-S-I-S-? wanting her thoughts on my health outlook.

"I really don't know at this time," Dr. G said, looking at me sadly.

Tears streamed down my cheeks as I stared at her, praying that she could fix me. "Find a cure. I'm a mom," I begged silently. Feeling let down, I shifted my gaze from her to the wall and cried. She touched my arm, gently squeezing it in a desperate attempt to console me, then left me alone in my room.

I'd been here for weeks, and no one had answers. I shook with fear. I redirected my gaze to the wall and saw my daughter. I cried, longing to kiss her sweet, soft head and hold her close. Dale looked over at me, sharing my pain.

Speech Therapy and Swallow Studies

That afternoon, my care team had scheduled another plasmapheresis treatment for me. As my previously used veins were already showing signs of distress, the nurses feared they would not hold up until the final round of plasmapheresis. Two young doctors were sent in with an ultrasound machine to find suitable veins and, as usual, Dale and Jared stood at my right side to support me.

To ease my anxiety, the doctors played "Don't Stop Believing" by Journey while they searched for veins, a gesture that was both sweet and surreal. They eventually found a suitable vein in my right arm, though they also discovered a blood clot and promptly started me on medication.

I indicated a wish to communicate with Jared and typed, T-O-M-O-R-R-O-W.

"What about tomorrow?" he asked.

I typed, S-C-H-E-D---. He interrupted me to say that he had missed a letter and asked me to start over. S-C-H-E-D-U-L-E T-O-M-O-R-R-O-W, I typed, slower.

"Oh, what's the schedule tomorrow?" Thumbs up. "Well, they will try sprinting again, and I know PT, OT, and speech therapy are planning on seeing you again."

Hearing the words "speech therapy" brought a rush of other questions, and I wasn't sure where to begin. This was my domain yet, as a school-based speech therapist, I didn't know a thing about this medically based field. Our worlds were very different. I worked with children who had never had communication skills, spending my days in classrooms and attending IEP meetings. Medical speech therapists, on the other hand, generally worked with patients who had lost their skills due to medical events, and spent their days in ICUs, rehab units, and participating in medical team rounds. Though we shared the same title, our environments and skillsets were vastly different. I was convinced I could never be a medical speech therapist.

I wondered what my speech therapy would entail. I typed, W-H-A-T W-I-L-L S-P-E-E-C-H D-O W-I-T-H M-E-? "What will speech do with me?" Jared repeated each word after I typed it. "What will they do with you?" He looked blankly at Dale. He took a breath, likely considering how he wanted to approach this conversation. In all likelihood, this was probably one of the more difficult conversations he generally had with a patient.

"We are having a speech therapist do a clinical swallow evaluation with you, once you are extubated. We want to see how your swallowing mechanism is working and if it is strong enough for you to start eating again. She may then recommend an instrumental swallow study called a modified barium swallow study also known as an MBSS to further assess your swallow function."

I remembered from grad school and my clinical internship that a modified barium swallow study is an X-ray test that shows how well someone can swallow. Different foods and liquids mixed with barium are swallowed, so the therapist can watch the process in real-time on a screen and check for any problems, like food or liquid going into the lungs.

Those were the words I was expecting to hear but certainly didn't want to hear because they meant that it probably wasn't safe for me to eat or drink anything by mouth, and my nasogastric (NG) tube feeding would need to continue.

When my medical condition had first deteriorated a few weeks ago, my medical team had placed an NG tube, and I had received all my nutrition and hydration via that tube, which I had always assumed would be a short-term arrangement.

My mind flashed back to grad school, completing barium trials for my dysphagia class, and thinking that was probably the first and last time I would ever have to taste barium. Now, here I was, actually facing the reality that I needed a modified barium swallow study done on myself.

I stared at them both and started to cry. Dale, at a loss for words, didn't respond, so Jared continued in his soft and compassionate tone, discussing the swallow study process.

Jared kept talking, and somehow, my focus gravitated back to the pictures on the wall. I stopped him mid-sentence and typed my daughter's name for both of them to see. I was done talking about swallow studies.

How was my daughter? Would someone please tell me how she was doing? Did she miss me? Would I ever see her again? I felt that if someone would just have communicated honestly with me and what she was doing on a daily basis, my anxiety would have lessened but I was left with only burning questions and fears. Both sensed that I needed to see her somehow, and she needed to know her mom was OK and fighting to be with her again. She needed to know I hadn't abandoned her.

Jared, sensing my deep sadness and longing to see her, offered to bring a social worker on to help me with all these worries. Emotionally drained from this conversation, I gave a thumbs up, signaling that I was done talking about this and wanted to be left alone.

Jared left the room, and I reflected on the conversation we had just had, feeling a huge sense of loss.

A Very Late Plasmapheresis Treatment

I looked at the clock and saw that it was 1:30 p.m. So far, nothing had gone my way today, and it reinforced in my mind that whatever was happening in my body was not good. I sat alone, reflecting on the conversation hours earlier with my team of doctors. I recalled them saying that they were going to do plasmapheresis today.

The whiteboard with my calendar of events said plasmapheresis at 1:00. The delay had me worried and raised questions in my mind. I inched my fingers toward my call button and hit it.

The nurse picked up and, knowing I couldn't talk, said, "I'll send the nurse in right away." Rachel walked in. Thankfully, my communication papers were lying on my lap, so I grabbed them and began typing. The process was slow. I typed, P-L-A-S-M-A--- and she cut me off.

"Plasmapheresis?" Rachel asked. I signaled, Y-E-S. She explained, "They are running behind schedule. I'll call them and see if they have a better approximation of when they will be starting."

I had further questions, but the thought of spelling it all out was just too exhausting, so instead, I hit the important points.

H-O-T, I typed. She walked over to the fan and moved it over right beside me so it was directly pointing at me. I could feel my legs perspiring beneath my bright yellow slip socks. I wiggled them in an attempt to get her attention. She picked up on my cue, walked over, and pushed them to the side.

T-H-A-N-K---. She stopped me halfway through. Rachel could now predict my thoughts. "You're welcome," she said and patted me on the leg. "Is there anything else that you need?" N-O, I typed and gave her the thumbs-up sign to express my gratitude.

It was now 3:00. They were two hours behind schedule. Was this procedure going to work? Would I wake up tomorrow feeling normal? Or, as the doctor said, possibly would nothing happen? Would this simply be a waste of everyone's time?

The curtain was pulled back and I hoped it was the nurse administering the plasmapheresis, but I was wrong. Jared was back to conduct his evening check-in before departing for the day.

I grabbed my communication papers, fully prepared to ask questions before he was gone for the night, knowing my safety blanket would be leaving. He brought up the plasmapheresis treatment, stating that they seemed to be running behind. W-H-A-T H-A-P-P-E-N-S I-F T-H-I-S D-O-E-S-N-'-T W-O-R-K-? I typed letter by letter, pausing between each word to ensure that he was understanding.

He repeated each word after I finished it, then paused, looking at Dale for clarification. Knowing I had lost both of them, I started over with my sentence. Internally I become frustrated and boiled with anger. Communicating like this was definitely one of the more frustrating aspects of my day.

He laughed jokingly and said, "You're just too fast of a typer, and I can't keep up." I felt bad for both of them because they meant well.

"What happens if this doesn't work?" he eventually got it, repeating my question. "We don't know whether it will work at all and we may not know if it is going to work for days, weeks, or possibly months. You will tell us if you notice any changes in the days ahead," he stated with a look of uncertainty.

I briefly closed my eyes, wanting to wake up from this bad dream. I opened them again when I heard the curtain pull back. A short woman appeared, pushing a large machine near my bed. She introduced herself and told me she would be administering my second plasmapheresis treatment. I anxiously grabbed my communication papers in preparation for answering any of her questions.

The heat in the room increased, and I kicked off the blankets. The compression socks squeezed my legs, and I felt my body stiffening up. She flushed the line out. It was a good sign when I tasted saline after the flush as it indicated that the vein was still in good shape. I felt a sense of relief that it worked but a lingering uncertainty about whether or not it would last the duration of the treatment. "Baby girl, Mama's coming home," I said to myself. I'll get better.

She walked over to the right side of my bed and followed the same procedure. Feeling trapped in bed, I inched my fingers over to grab my communication papers. I typed, H-O-T, F-A-N. She pointed the fan at me. It did not do much, but I appreciated the gesture. She turned it up.

The nurse left the room, and it was quiet for a brief moment. My gaze looked left, and I could see the sun starting to set. But the day wasn't over for me. It was just starting in some respects. The clock read 7:05 p.m. It was shift change.

Rachel walked back into the room to say her goodnight. She looked at me and saw tears in my eyes. "Vanessa, you're a fighter. You're going to get out of here, but don't give up!" She gently touched my arm. Deeply grateful for her kindness and sensitivity but terrified to have her leave, I wanted to reach out and hug her but couldn't. I was wrapped under the weight of tubes tethered to machines. I typed, T-H-A-N-K Y-O-U.

"Of course," she said. She noticed that my head had fallen to the right and quickly rolled up the towels and stuffed them once again behind my ear. She stepped back to check the alignment and asked, "Is that OK?" I gave her a thumbs up as she left.

I was alone again and my mind wandered. What if this doesn't work – what's their next plan? What if the veins don't hold up? Dale had to leave. I was tired. Who was my next nurse? Panic. I looked down at my arms covered in tubes and saw those two fresh IV lines inserted into my arms, and I cried. I cried for all the time I was losing with my daughter by sitting here fighting for my life.

Beep, beep, beep. The machine blared. The short nurse stood up and pushed the button on the machine. She proceeded to walk over to me and adjust my arms. "You'll need to keep them as straight as possible," she said. Knowing that I couldn't move my arm, she kindly adjusted it for me. She walked over to push some buttons on the machine, whose rhythmic humming told me it was working.

My room was dark, with only a few lights on the machine lighting up. I laid in my bed, as stiff as a board, unable to move, tubes tangled all around my arms. How can someone as healthy as I was become so terribly sick? Was I too stressed and doing too much and my body just wore out?

I woke up to the short nurse moving the plastic IV tube that was draped over my chest and around my arms. I was grateful that it was over and that my veins had held up.

Rachel came in and notified me that I would have nurse Laura again as she said her final farewell for the day.

Laura entered the room, her blonde hair neatly pulled back, and she offered me a warm smile. She quickly assessed the situation, checking my vitals with practiced efficiency.

"How are you doing tonight, Vanessa?" she asked, her voice gentle yet matter of fact.

I gave her a thumbs up and typed, R-E-L-I-E-V-E-D T-O S-E-E Y-O-U on my communication papers.

"Glad to hear that," she responded, squeezing my hand reassuringly. "Let's get you comfortable and go over the plan for tonight."

Laura explained the evening's procedures, her tone filled with empathy and encouragement. As she adjusted my pillow and towel rolls and ensured my call button was within reach, I felt a wave of gratitude. Her attention to detail and genuine concern for my well-being made such a world of difference.

She commented on the pictures on the wall, noticing that new ones had recently been added. I looked at her and started to cry. The stress and worry were just too much.

"Yeah, I know you miss your girl." She reassured me that they were working hard to figure this all out so I could go home. "Let me get you some Ativan to help you sleep." I was just happy to have someone listening to me to help take the edge off.

She walked away and closed the curtain behind her. Within a minute, she was back, holding a short, clear plastic tube in her hand. "This should help you sleep," she said. She took the cap off. Never in a million years would I have allowed this medication into my body on a typical day but, for some reason, my mind wasn't thinking about the damaging effects of medications. I wanted out, and this was the answer at this time.

A Desperate Late Night Phone Call

At 4:20 a.m., I woke up again. It was dark but I knew there was someone in my room. I could see the outline of their body walking back and forth, touching the ventilator machine to my left. What were they doing? Was my machine functioning properly? Why would someone be here at this hour? What was wrong? I couldn't ask. With the room dark, no one knew I was awake. I panicked and couldn't tame my worry. The person left and now I couldn't go back to sleep.

I reached for my call button, desperate for more sleep medication, but it was nowhere to be found. My left hand moved the tubes, but I couldn't find the button. I shook free of all the blankets, but it was gone. I started trembling. I needed help. I used my left hand to bang the side of my bed, hoping someone would hear me. I banged harder and louder, but no one came. Feeling hot, I kicked off the blankets.

I couldn't talk, but I could call out on my phone. However, I didn't know the nursing station's number. No one I knew was up at this hour to receive a text. I could call my parents' landline but would've hated to wake them, even though I knew they would be the only ones who would answer. They wouldn't know the nurses' number either.

My last attempt was to call Dale. He never had his phone on, but maybe this once he would have it on. I hit the speed dial, and it rang and rang and rang. I reached to hang up, but then he answered. I pressed buttons, one after another, random numbers, one after another, signaling that I was there, I was alive. I desperately needed help, but couldn't communicate it. Beep, beep, beep. "Vanessa, text me," he said.

"Call nurses. I need help. Can't find call button," I texted frantically. Shaking and crying, I hung up. Within a minute, the door opened, and Laura walked through. Relieved, I realized that Dale had reached them. I typed, C-A-N-'-T F-I-N-D C-A-L-L B-U-T-T-O-N. She scanned the bed, lifted pillows, and then looked down to find it lying on the floor.

"Here you go," she said with a smile. "Are you OK?" Tearfully, I typed, I-'-M S-C-A-R-E-D. My lifeline to the world was back on my lap, but I felt so alone and scared, I needed more sleep meds. I needed to sleep, but she wouldn't give me more at this point as I had hit my nightly limit.

Feeling heartbroken and enraged, I desperately needed to talk. I was sick of the slow, frustrating process of typing out words, knowing there were better options available. I couldn't believe they didn't have an iPad with an AAC app; it was 2019! Then it hit me – I could use my phone. I quickly downloaded a text-to-speech app from the App Store. I couldn't believe I hadn't thought of this before.

The next morning Dale and Jared entered my room at the perfect time. With some optimism and feeling a sense of progress was finally being made, I looked at them both and picked up my phone, opened the app, typed in "Good morning" from my phone, and hit "enter." Seeing their relieved smiles as the app spoke for me, we all felt a wave of progress and a glimmer of hope.

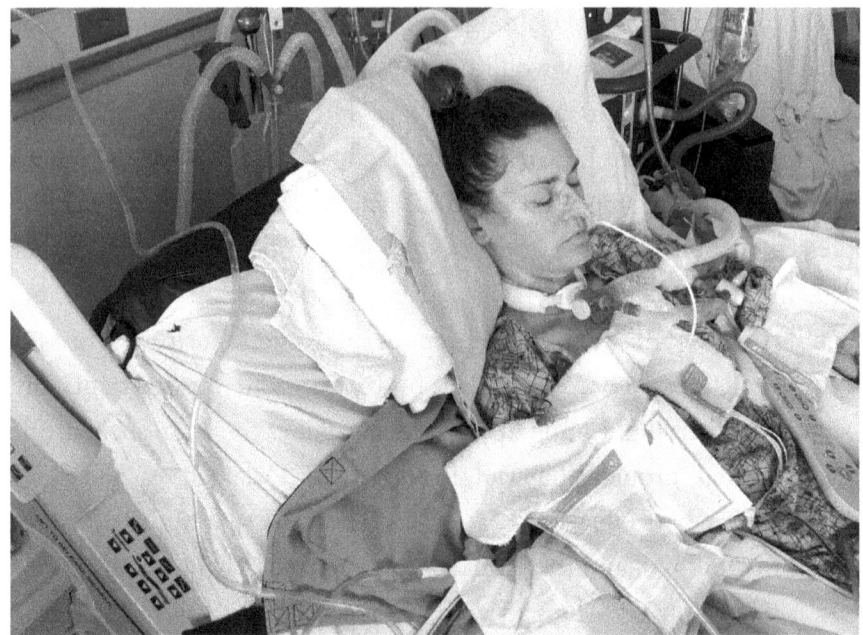

UCSD ICU

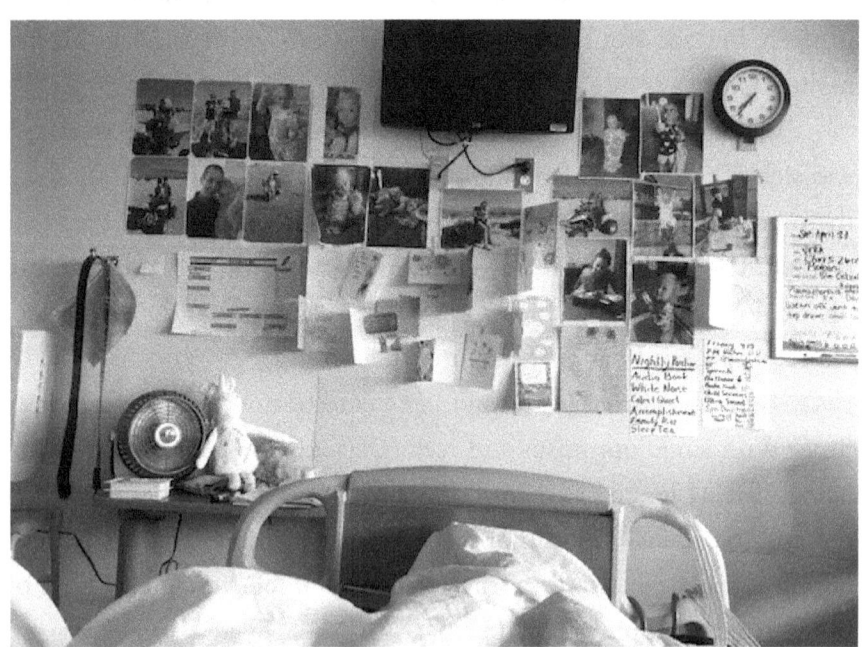

My ICU room decorated at UCSD

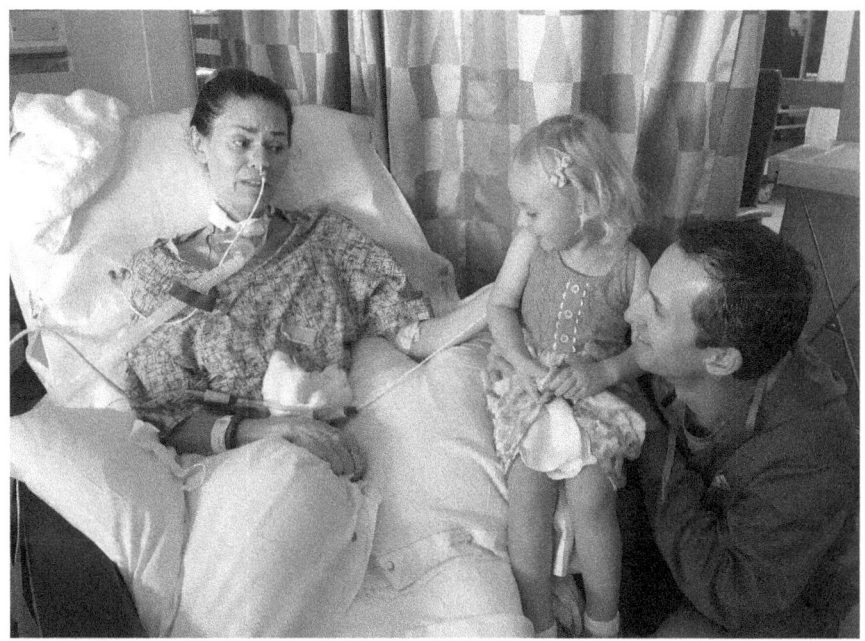

My daughter's first visit to the ICU

My UCSD ICU team of nurses

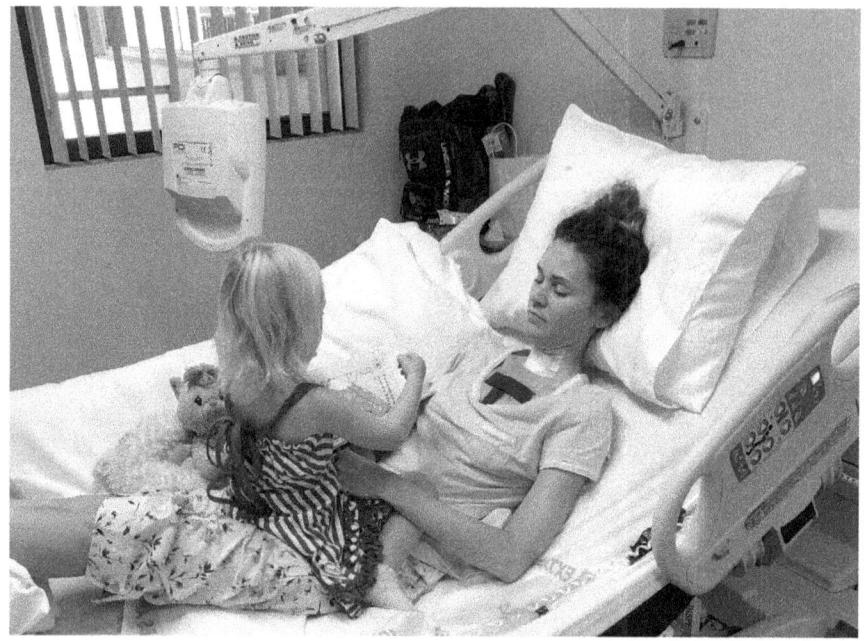

My daughter visiting me at Desert Regional rehab

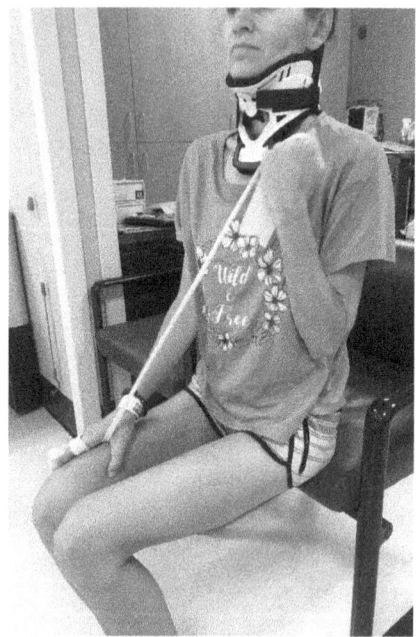

Desert Regional OT session

Me with my outpatient SLP Sherry after my final therapy session

Dr. Rosen, Dale and I

Jess, Tara and I hiking at the beach

Dr. Rosen, nurse Cat, nurse Laura and I at the beach

My first time driving with my dad

Dana and my mom holding me up as I returned to work

My daugher and I taking our nap together

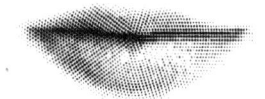

CHAPTER 7
More Losses and Small Gains

Dale arrived that morning, his arms full of packages of cookies and muffins. It was a gesture he frequently made to show the staff how much we appreciated them taking us under their wing and providing exceptional care. He placed the treats at the nurses' station, greeting each staff member with a heartfelt "Thank you" as he checked the board to see who my day nurse would be. This small act of kindness was his way of expressing our gratitude for their constant support and dedication.

A Speaking Valve

I had been on mechanical ventilation for 14 days now, following my initial decline at my first ICU. I was tolerating my tracheostomy well and my speech therapist, Lindsey, decided it was time to see if I could begin vocalizations and tolerate anything orally. She introduced me to something called a Passy-Muir Valve, a speaking valve, and explained how it worked. She told me that since I now had a tracheostomy, I was breathing through the stoma, or hole, at the base of my neck and that the air went in and out of that stoma. That stoma was below my vocal folds, so I had no voice because the air bypassed my vocal folds entirely.

"Normally, when you speak, air from your lungs passes through your vocal folds, causing them to vibrate and produce sound," she explained, her tone patient and empathetic. "But with a tracheostomy, the air doesn't reach your vocal folds because it exits through the stoma, or the hole in your throat, instead."

She showed me the small, cylindrical Passy-Muir Valve. "This valve will help you speak," she continued. "When we place it over your tracheostomy tube, it allows air to enter through the stoma as you inhale. But when you exhale, the valve closes and redirects the air up through your vocal folds, causing them to vibrate and produce sound."

Her explanation was thorough yet gentle, as she understood how overwhelming all of this was for me. "When we place the speaking valve on the outside of your trache that gives you the ability to produce voice via this valve, it is a one-way valve by rerouting the exhaled air through your vocal cords, enabling you to speak. It's an incredible tool that will help you regain your voice."

She demonstrated how to use the valve, placing it gently over my tracheostomy tube. I felt a slight resistance as I breathed out, and then, for the first time since the surgery, I heard a faint sound escape my lips. It wasn't much, but it was a start.

"This will take some getting used to," she reassured me, "but with practice, you'll find it easier to use each session. We'll work on this together, and I'll be here to support you every step of the way."

Her confidence and the presence of the speaking valve boosted my hope. I nodded, feeling a mixture of apprehension and determination. The journey ahead was daunting, but knowing I had tools like the speaking valve and supportive professionals by my side made it seem a little more manageable.

She gently placed the speaking valve on my tracheostomy, twisted it into place and described to me what I would feel as I tried to vocalize for the first time.

Using the speaking valve for the first time was uncomfortable and exhausting. Multiple times, I coughed up thick secretions that tasted bitter and disgusting. The smell was awful as well. The effort required to speak was immense, involving muscles that had been dormant for so long. Each breath felt like a marathon, my chest heaving with the exertion. My initial vocalization was a long and labored "ahhhhh," and the sound was strained and weak. It took every ounce of strength to force air past the valve, my throat burning with the effort. I coughed, my body flailing uncontrollably as I spewed up secretion after secretion. The taste was vividly unpleasant and, after a few minutes, I was utterly spent, my energy completely drained.

My goal was to vocalize for eight seconds and I had failed miserably. My hands trembled from the effort, and I felt lightheaded. Begging to remove the valve, I realized just how monumental the task of regaining my voice would be. The experience left me feeling more defeated than ever, wondering if I would ever truly regain my voice.

Even though it was a struggle, the speaking valve gave me my voice back and I was no longer speechless. I no longer needed to rely on my communication papers or my communication board.

My tolerance for the speaking valve was low though and I couldn't wear it for long periods of time. The valve also caused me to have increased sensations of my secretions. I could feel them clogging my airway resulting in constant coughing and a feeling of suffocation. Dale's shoulders slumped a little more each time he watched me struggle to manage secretions and speak. He kept encouraging me, whispering words of support, but I could feel the weight of his disappointment mingling with my own despair.

A Bedside Swallow Evaluation

Lindsey's explanations felt hard to grasp, as if they were coming from a place far removed from my reality. Being a school-based speech therapist had made it difficult for me to understand the details of her instructions. The world of a medically based speech therapist was foreign to me and so were the team members. For this assessment, a respiratory therapist was also in the room for the speaking valve tolerance, but more importantly, to manage the inflating and deflating of the tracheostomy cuff.

The bedside swallow test was fairly simple. The ice chips and cup of water she held were meant to test my swallowing reflexes, a small yet significant step in my therapy. If I were able to swallow those, then she would test additional items. I watched her closely, her calm demeanor a stark contrast to the storm of emotions within me.

Despite my fear and confusion, I gave her my full attention and did what she instructed me to do, determined to show that I was committed to my recovery. Voices in the back of my mind urged me to remain cooperative and show appreciation for all she was doing. I didn't want to be the speech therapist who gave up, was rude, or – worst of all – showed a lack of desire to improve.

She picked up a small piece of ice from the cup and gently brought it to my mouth. As an SLP, I had an inkling of what this was about, but the specifics were unclear to me. I placed my trust in her expertise, knowing she wouldn't want any patient, let alone another SLP, to face severe complications like aspiration under her watch.

The ice touched my tongue, and I began to suck on it. She placed her fingers on my throat and instructed me to swallow the slowly melting ice. The sensation triggered memories of my grad school days when I had performed similar tests on patients. She repeated the process with another small piece of crushed ice, placing her fingers on my throat again to gauge my swallowing ability. I couldn't decipher her exact findings, but her body language spoke volumes.

After setting the cup aside, she gently explained to both of us that my swallowing function was severely compromised. She explained that, while she couldn't see what was happening in my throat, there were indications that my swallow was too slow and weak and that the melted ice had not been safely swallowed.

I gripped my communication papers tightly. Knowing I had something to say, she moved in closer and watched intensely. My fingers shaking, I typed, W-H-A-T-'-S N-E-X-T-?

She looked at me with gentle eyes and said, "I'll give you a list of exercises to do each day to help strengthen your muscles. After some time, we'll likely want to do a barium swallow study to see how you are progressing. But for now, I can't recommend eating orally," she said, giving me a look that knew I would be sad about this news.

Exhausted, I gave her a thumbs-up sign, indicating that I had understood, but not relaying the sheer fear boiling inside of me. I looked her in the eyes, tears trickling down my face in hopes of conveying to her how vulnerable and scared I was. She left the room and, as she closed the curtain behind her, I continued to cry for all that I had lost and in fear of what was to come.

Dale trailed closely behind Lindsey as she left, and I was left alone in the quiet of my room. As I laid there, I couldn't help but reflect on the conversation with Lindsey. It was clear that grad school had not prepared me for the emotional challenges of working with a fellow SLP, especially in such a personal and vulnerable context. The reality of being on the receiving end of therapy, particularly from someone in my own profession, was an emotional weight I never anticipated.

The clock in front of me read 3:15, and I found myself wishing desperately for some medication to put me to sleep so I could forget all that just happened. I was trapped in a nightmare I couldn't escape.

A Test to Assess My Swallow and a Feeding Tube

For almost two weeks now, I had been receiving all my nutrition and medications through a tube connecting with my stomach. This was not a long-term option, and when it became apparent that I was not going to be able to eat or drink safely anytime soon, my speech therapist recommended that I complete an instrumental swallowing assessment called a Modified Barium Swallow Study. She explained that she wanted to see the nature of my swallowing difficulties and to see if any swallowing strategies or positioning strategies would improve my overall safety of oral intake.

It took a team of people to get me out of bed and into a "swallow chair". Dale took charge of holding my head up as the neck brace was wrapped around my head. It was ill-fitting, still requiring towels for additional support. I hated it with passion and longed for the day I no longer needed it.

As my nurse pushed me down the hallway, Dale at her side, I stared forward not saying a word.

In the Radiology Department, I was transferred to a "swallow chair" made specifically for this study. It was hard, uncomfortable, cold, and very narrow. I had to sit in a certain position and not move too much, as this position and stillness were needed for the "best pictures."

Everyone in the room had on large lead radiation vests, thyroid protectors, and little square boxes called dosimeters that measured their radiation level. No little box for me. I had nothing but a little lead apron for my lap, my hospital gown, and a thin blanket. I felt vulnerable, exposed, and terrified. What if I failed this test? What if I could never eat or drink again? How would I ever make it through a family dinner again, much less a holiday meal? I was lost in anxious thoughts.

I sat in the chair, as Lindsey prepared to conduct the swallow trials. Following the Modified Barium Swallow Impairment Protocol, she was prepared for a full set of trials. On a tray beside the fluoroscopy machine, she had prepared trials including thin, nectar thick, and moderately thick liquids and pureed, soft, and crunchy food, all mixed with barium.

She explained that a fluoroscopy machine is like a video X-ray machine and that as I swallowed the trials, she would be able to see where they were going because she could watch the barium. I remember her telling me that she would be looking to see whether anything went into my lungs when I swallowed, and if it did, what we could do about that. Overall, I knew that she was hoping, like I was, that I'd be able to start eating and drinking again.

She explained that first, she would start with one teaspoon sip of liquid barium for the fluoroscopy machine. She knew that I was in pain, sitting there in a stiff and tight neck brace with impaired muscles. It was far from comfortable, but she did her best to keep me at ease. The room was dimly lit, shadows dancing on the walls, and I couldn't see what she was seeing on the screen. The darkness added to the feeling of isolation and vulnerability.

Tears streamed down my cheeks as I reflected back to grad school, remembering when I had learned about this very procedure. The irony was almost unbearable; I had once been the one studying the techniques and now, I was the patient, struggling to perform basic functions. My neck ached from the brace, my muscles were weak, and every swallow felt like an insurmountable task.

The discomfort was overwhelming, both physically and emotionally, and the tears continued to flow as I grappled with the harsh reality of my situation. I was so hot, and there was nothing to cool me down, so I had to focus and get this done.

The room was dark, and I couldn't see what Lindsey was seeing on the screen. I wondered what the study was showing.

As I tried to swallow, I felt an odd sensation, a misdirection of sorts. It became clear something was wrong. My heart sank as I noticed the concerned look on Lindsey's face. She gave me another trial of liquid barium and again, I felt that same misdirection, an alarming awareness that the substance was not going down the right way.

After only a few trials of the barium liquid, Lindsey decided to stop, and I immediately knew things weren't going well. She looked at me with apprehension and sadness in her eyes, saying my swallow was still too weak.

The harsh reality hit me when she explained that I had aspirated my trials, meaning that what Lindsey gave me went into my lungs instead of my stomach. She further explained that the risk of pneumonia from aspiration while eating and drinking was high due to the weakness of my swallow. She gently and slowly explained that she was recommending I consider the stomach feeding tube and nothing orally at this time.

I felt a wave of despair wash over me as I realized just how far I was from being able to eat or drink normally again. The fear of developing pneumonia added another layer to my already overwhelming anxiety, and I couldn't help but feel defeated by yet another setback in my recovery.

They took me back to my room, and I asked to be transferred to my chair. I was determined to sit in my bedside chair as much as I could tolerate and to avoid being in bed as much as possible, because I knew being in the chair was a far better option at this point. Sitting upright in the chair helped with my breathing and speaking, and mentally it made me feel a bit more human and less like a patient confined to a hospital bed. Every time I managed to stay in the chair for a while, it felt like a small victory in a battle that often seemed overwhelming.

Back in my room, Lindsey gave me a list of swallowing exercises to do such as Masako maneuvers and Mendelsohn exercises. She explained that the Masako maneuver is a swallowing exercise used to strengthen the muscles of the throat, particularly the base of the tongue. She then modeled it for me by gently holding her tongue between her teeth and swallowing. She said this engages the muscles in the back of your throat more intensely., improving the efficiency of my swallow.

She then demonstrated, the Mendelsohn maneuver and explained that this swallowing exercise was designed to improve swallowing coordination and help prevent aspiration.

She explained that I was instructed to swallow normally and, in the middle of the swallow, to try and hold my Adam's apple up as long as I could, almost like I was pausing in the act of swallowing. I tried it myself, feeling my throat muscles engage and then attempting to sustain the elevation. It felt awkward and unnatural at first, but she assured me that with practice, it could strengthen the muscles involved in swallowing and improve my ability to safely swallow without food or liquid going down the wrong way.

She demonstrated how to do them both again, and I performed them diligently, hoping to improve. As she left, Dale followed behind her, eager to ask further questions about my prognosis without me hearing.

She updated him with delicately chosen words, her voice tinged with sadness as she conveyed the gravity and severity of my situation. It must have been a heart-wrenching conversation for both of them, grappling with the stark contrast between their hopes and the harsh realities of my condition.

I continued to do the exercises independently and continually hit my call button, requesting additional suctioning. I struggled to breathe.

Dale's disappointment mirrored my own. He tried to mask his feelings, but I could see the pain in his eyes. He wanted so desperately for these exercises to work, to see even the smallest sign of progress, but day after day, it just wasn't happening.

Due to my aspirant events during the swallow study and slow progress with the bedside exercises, the decision was made to proceed with a stomach feeding tube, or PEG tube, for nutrition. The NG tube was at risk of causing an infection, so the PEG tube had become necessary. It seemed like I was going backward instead of forward.

The decision filled me with panic. The thought of another invasive procedure was overwhelming. My mind raced with fear and anxiety about the unknown. Would it hurt? Would there be complications?

The idea of having a feeding tube inserted into my stomach was horrifying. I couldn't shake the image of the doctors cutting into me, the cold instruments, and the sterile hospital room. My heart pounded in my chest, but I knew this was necessary and could not be avoided.

The PEG tube placement was a painful ordeal. Though I was given local anesthesia, I could feel the pressure on my abdomen and hear the voices of the doctors as they cut into me. The pain afterward was intense, far surpassing anything I had ever experienced – including childbirth. As a result, I was in need of powerful narcotics once again.

I watched the clock closely and made sure to notify the nurse every four hours when I was due for my next dose of pain relief. As soon as the medication was administered, a wave of relief would wash over me and I was released from the pain. It was a profound and surreal experience – one that made me understand why people might become dependent on these drugs. The relief was so complete and immediate that it transported me far from my pain and worries, if only for a short while.

Feeding through the PEG tube brought its own set of challenges. Nausea, bloating, and feverish chills were common due to rushes of anxiety. I was plagued with fears about the tube malfunctioning or the nurses not knowing how to use it. Because I had lost so much weight, I was given a pediatric tube, which many of the nurses were unfamiliar with. My need for nutrition was critical for survival and leaving that in the hands of others terrified me. Relying on others unfamiliar with my tube to keep me alive and fed filled me with anxiety.

Each time they connected the tube, I couldn't help but worry if they were doing it correctly. I imagined worst-case scenarios, like the tube malfunctioning or causing an infection and having to rely on the NG tube again. Each feeding would cause my body to sweat with the rise in anxiety. My mind was constantly racing, and although there were never any infections, the fear continued.

My survival depended on their knowledge and competence, and the stakes felt incredibly high. I had to trust that they would keep me alive and fed, but that trust was hard to muster amidst my fears of not having control. Despite these anxieties, the NG tube was eventually removed once the PEG tube was functioning well.

However, my anxiety remained – a constant companion as I navigated this new reality. The PEG tube represented a lifeline, but also a source of relentless worry. The nurses were kind and patient, but their lack of familiarity with the pediatric tube was evident, and I couldn't help but feel like a burden.

As the days passed, I slowly began to adapt to the routine. The nurses became more comfortable with the tube, and my anxiety, while still present, began to lessen. However, the bloating continued. We later discovered that the ingredients in the feeding formula were not real food but a mixture of unpronounceable chemicals in disguise. The nutritionist offered us an alternative tube feed to try that was organic and filled with real food ingredients. The bloating quickly dissipated. This change brought immense relief and made the feeding process much more manageable.

The removal of the NG tube was a milestone, a sign that I was making progress, however small. But the journey was far from over, and I knew that I had to continue fighting, one day at a time.

Each day was a struggle filled with medical procedures and the constant fight to regain some semblance of normalcy. The journey was far from over, but with each new procedure completed, I found renewed determination to keep pushing forward, driven by the images of my daughter on the wall and the unwavering support of Dale and Jared.

Dale continued to update my list of accomplishments daily on the wall. He now added the following:

- Tolerated the speaking valve for three minutes
- Completed three rounds of plasmapheresis treatments
- Underwent tracheostomy surgery
- Received a PEG tube

The list of accomplishments was noteworthy, and my nursing team kept reminding me of that. However, in the back of my mind, I wondered if I would be able to accomplish and survive the day Jared left our side. I knew his graduation was approaching, and thus his final day in the ICU as well, and that weighed heavily on my heart and mind. What would we do without him?

I had grown so accustomed to his presence and support that I wasn't sure I would be able to persevere.

Each day was a struggle, filled with medical procedures and the constant fight to regain some semblance of normalcy. The journey was far from over, but with each setback, I found a renewed determination to keep pushing forward, driven by the images of my daughter on the wall and the unwavering support of Dale and Jared.

PT/OT Session

The day started off with an early morning session of PT and OT. Knowing that I was under insurmountable stress, battling depression, and needing a change of scenery, Jess looked at me and said, "What would you think about going outside today?" I looked at her, wondering what that would be like, but I trusted she knew what she was doing. "It's a beautiful day, and I think going outside would do you some good."

She gathered the team, and everyone circled around my bedside, resuming their positions for transferring me from my bed to the wheelchair as I was still fully dependent on everyone around me for transfers. Dale was responsible for holding my head as they strategically placed the cumbersome and dreaded neck brace around my neck.

As they pushed me out of the comfort zone of my ICU room where I was surrounded by the familiar sounds and smells that had become my refuge, panic began to set in. I was not prepared to leave this environment. My body began to sweat and tremble with fear, but I fought to keep my anxiety hidden. In some ways, I longed to be outside, to see something new and tackle a new goal in a different setting. But the sudden shift felt overwhelming, like the world was rushing forward while I was still trying to catch my breath. The change was happening too fast, and I was scared.

As they wheeled me into the elevator, the familiar walls of the ICU faded away, replaced by a growing sense of unease. When the doors opened to the lobby, I was greeted by a bustling space where people came and went—checking in to visit loved ones or attend appointments, I wasn't really sure. As they pushed me through the crowd, I felt incredibly self-conscious, as if every pair of eyes was fixed on me. It didn't matter that I was just another patient in a hospital filled with others in wheelchairs and on gurneys; the attention felt suffocating. Panic swirled inside me, intensified by the fear of leaving the comfort of my room. I longed to be outside, to experience something new and work toward a new goal, yet everything was happening too fast, and I was scared.

Jess found a quiet spot at a bench where I could sit in the sun. The warmth on my skin felt comforting after being inside for so long. A light breeze brushed against my face, and it felt so surreal—something I had missed deeply without even realizing it. Being outside on the bench, surrounded by the sounds of nature, the breeze, and the sunshine began to calm my anxiety. It was a surreal experience. Refreshing and invigorating, a gentle reminder of the outside world I had longed for while confined within the sterile walls of the hospital.

Jess didn't need to bring any therapy materials, as I was not in need of anything—my body was so frail and weak. The focus was simply to get me outside in a new environment to stimulate my senses. We worked on postural and trunk control, gently adjusting my position to help me engage my core and stabilize my movements. She sat beside me, watching my every movement for correct form and safety while guiding my right arm, which was unable to move on its own. She provided hand-over-hand assistance to help retrain it, encouraging me to practice sliding it forward and backward along the table in front of me, the weight of it feeling heavy and weak.

The warmth of the sun and the gentle breeze made each small effort feel more significant, as if I was reconnecting with a part of myself that had been dormant for too long. Dale stood nearby, watching intently. His face was a mix of hope and concern, silently willing my muscles to respond. Jess adjusted my arm, positioning it to try another exercise. My arm trembled with the effort, barely moving, but she smiled and encouraged me not to give up. I appreciated her enthusiasm and positivity.

As Jess gently told me it was time to go back, I felt a wave of sadness wash over me at the thought of returning to the familiar hospital walls I had grown so accustomed to. Being outside had momentarily allowed me to forget all the medical trauma I had endured over the past few weeks, and now the thought of going back felt like losing a small piece of that newfound freedom.

Jess looked at me, her eyes reflecting a mixture of sadness for what I had been through, yet also a glimmer of hope. Despite everything, she recognized and acknowledged my fighting spirit, speaking with a warmth and positivity that made me feel seen and understood. She then turned to Dale, gratitude evident in her voice, and thanked him for the unwavering support he had shown, not just to me, but also to her during our trip outside. His presence had made a difference, and Jess made sure he knew it.

Jared Calls My Parents

Recognizing my mounting anxiety about my daughter and parents visiting me, Jared stepped in and volunteered to call my parents and prep them for the visit. He offered to discuss the procedures I had undergone and my current prognosis, as well as to answer any questions they might have.

This gesture significantly relieved some of my anxiety.

I knew my parents deserved to understand what I was going through, and having Jared provide them with detailed information felt like a weight had been lifted from my shoulders. Dale texted my parents and set up a time for Jared to talk to them.

Jared spent about an hour on the phone with them, patiently explaining everything. My parents were incredibly grateful for the time and effort he took to address their concerns, which in turn eased my worries. However, he also reminded me that he would be graduating soon and would, therefore, no longer be coming in for my daily checkups and wouldn't be available for the emotional support I had grown accustomed to.

A Pink Blanket for My Daughter

Knowing that I was hyper-focused on seeing my family again for the first time in nearly three weeks, my occupational therapist brought me a kit for a "tie blanket" which was a bright pink adorned with beautiful orange, green, and white flowers. The task during therapy was to tie the blanket together, a project designed to help with fine motor skills. But it wasn't just a therapy exercise; it was also meant to become a heartfelt gift for my daughter when she visited.

As I sat in the chair, tying each knot as best I could with only one working hand, I felt a surge of happiness. Knowing that I was creating something special for my daughter, something pink that she would love, gave me a sense of purpose and joy.

However, a significant concern loomed over me. How would she react to seeing me covered in medical tubes? I didn't want to appear scary to her. I was determined to tolerate my speaking valve for longer periods because I wanted to speak to her and avoid using text-to-speech.

My team tried to find ways to cover the tubes. They brought an oversized shirt, hoping it would mask the tubes. Putting it on was cumbersome, requiring careful maneuvering to avoid dislodging any of the medical equipment. The process was slow. With each movement, I held my breath as they tried to slip the shirt over my head without disturbing the connections. We quickly realized that the shirt, despite our best efforts, wasn't going to work.

Ultimately, we decided to drape a sheet over the tubes to hide them from view yet still keep them accessible. We tried our best to conceal them while ensuring that everything remained secure. It didn't entirely mask the reality of my condition, but it gave me a semblance of dignity and a tiny bit of comfort.

Speech Therapy Continues

Speech therapy sessions continued daily with Lindsey at my side. She was relentless, focusing on my use of my voice and my tolerance of the speaking valve for longer periods of time. In anticipation of my family coming to visit, I pushed myself harder and harder, hoping to avoid using text-to-speech and to appear as normal as possible upon their arrival.

I never imagined the act of learning to speak again would be so physically exhausting. We also focused on improving the strength of my swallowing through swallowing exercises and trials with ice chips.

Despite efforts, the secretions remained a problem, necessitating frequent suctioning. Due to the nature of my disease, I produced a higher level of secretions than normal, so they offered me a Yankauer suctioning tool to provide additional suctioning on an as-needed basis.

I clung to the suctioning device, and it hardly ever left my hand. Without it I feared I would choke on my own secretions and die. I frantically kept it close to me, along with my phone for communication if needed.

Communicating remained challenging, and I often relied on text-to-speech technology to give myself a much-needed break from the exhausting effort required by the speaking valve.

The frustration of not making progress with my swallowing exercises, like the Mendelsohn and Masako maneuvers, was becoming unbearable. Day in and day out, I performed these exercises both with my therapist and independently but was still designated as NPO (not able to take anything by mouth) and could only suck on ice chips. The lack of noticeable improvement was disheartening to everyone and deepened my depression.

In preparation for my daughter's visit, Lindsey gave me an assignment to record a video message for her before she visited. It was meant to help her not only see me in my condition but also hear my new voice. To record the message, I carefully positioned the phone, holding it up with my left hand, while also attempting to hide the trache tubes, capturing only my face.

I painstakingly composed a message, saying, "Hi honey, it's Mommy. I miss you so much! I can't wait to see you. I'll see you tomorrow. I love you so, so, so much." My voice sounded nasally and different, a far cry from the voice she was used to. I hoped that hearing me would bring her some comfort in anticipation for her arrival the next day.

I put the phone down and watched my video, tears running down my face in sadness as I saw myself in the images for the first time. I looked so sad, depleted, and frightened. My smile was now forced and fake. My skin and hair color were not the same as they once were. The stress I had endured was definitely showing after three weeks.

A First Visit from My Daughter

UCSD has a dedicated team called Child Life that specializes in working with children of patients who are hospitalized. They take a family-centered approach to care and work with a multidisciplinary team to ensure that the social, emotional and psychological needs are being met for the children of adult patients.

They offered to come and transform the room to make it more child-friendly and welcoming, a gesture I truly appreciated since my biggest concern was ensuring my daughter felt at ease in this environment. The team not only covered up the intimidating medical machines but also brought toys like Thomas the Train and Peppa Pig characters to keep her distracted and entertained. They even laid down a brightly colored foam mat, providing a much more comfortable and inviting spot for her to sit compared to the cold, sterile hospital floor.

Everyone on my team was aware of my anxiety about my daughter and my parents visiting in the next few days and did their best to prepare me and my environment for their arrival. All I wanted was to be given the gift of holding my baby again.

I was sitting up in the chair more frequently. It was a significant milestone, and I was proud of my progress, even though it required a team effort to get me into the chair. I knew being in bed wasn't going to help me achieve my goals.

However, transitioning from the bed to the chair was a major challenge, requiring the coordinated effort of four people to manage the neck brace and carefully move me. So I decided to stay in bed for her arrival.

They understood the emotional rollercoaster I was on and worked tirelessly to prepare me for the visit, aiming to keep my anxiety at bay.

The next day, my parents and daughter arrived in town. They had driven down and stayed about 15-20 minutes away from the hospital. As they arrived at UCSD, they texted Dale, who went outside to meet them and walked them in. As Dale left to bring them in, a wave of panic set in. Was this really happening? I was terrified of how my daughter would react upon seeing me. I envisioned her fear and confusion, worried that the sight of me would be too much for her. My greatest fear was she wouldn't remember me and that she wouldn't want me to hold her.

I heard Dale enter the ICU unit before I saw him. I knew he had our daughter with him. He soon pulled back the curtains and entered. He was holding my daughter tightly in his arms. The sight of her little body was almost too painful to bear. I wanted so desperately to hold her but also knew what a risk it was with all the tubes covering my body.

My parents filed into the room as well and looked at me, and at their granddaughter a look of sadness and uncertainty on their faces. I knew they were trying their best to be optimistic and positive saying how good I looked compared to their last time seeing me. I knew everyone around me was scared for me but they all tried their best to hide their true emotions, not to worry me or my daughter.

As Dale and my daughter entered the room, she stared at me, reluctant to come closer. She clung tightly to her dad, her little arms wrapped around his neck, finding comfort in his familiar presence. Seeing me, her mother, in such an unfamiliar state was understandably frightening for her. My heart sank. I wanted desperately to stand up, and give her a comforting hug that said, "I'll be home soon," but I wasn't entirely sure of that myself.

Nervously, I looked at her and smiled. "Hi, honey!" I said, using my speaking valve. I wanted so badly for her to come sit on my lap but I was afraid I might drop her or that she might accidentally pull my trache tube out or dislodge other necessary equipment.

She looked at me with a mix of curiosity and confusion as the yellow feeding tube hung out of my nose. In an attempt to not scare her and to ease her worries, he gently said, "Honey, look, it's a noodle in Mommy's nose." This simple explanation was his way of making the situation less frightening and more understandable for her. Despite the seriousness of the moment, his words were meant to preserve her sense of normalcy and protect her from the more daunting aspects of my condition. It was a touching example of the lengths we went to ensure that she felt safe and secure, even as I navigated through my own struggles.

In an effort to bridge the gap, I gave her the blanket I had made OT, remembering painstakingly how long it had taken me to tie each knot. Despite an overwhelming sense of grief, I forced myself to display a positive and happy attitude. I didn't want anyone to worry about me, least of all my daughter. I wanted her to see me as strong and OK, even though inside, I was struggling with embarrassment, exhaustion, and a deep feeling of loss. My heart was breaking for all of our losses.

The Child Life team went above and beyond, bringing in a surprise – matching brown teddy bears for her and me. These teddy bears were not ordinary; they were rigged to resemble my medical situation, complete with traches, IV lines, and tubes.

The intention was to desensitize her to my condition, showing her that the teddy bear, much like her mom, had similar features and was still just a teddy bear. When I saw the teddy bears, I fought back tears. It was an incredibly touching gesture that made the harsh reality a little bit easier to take.

With hesitation, Dale gently placed my daughter on my lap. I touched her little hand and kissed her forehead as I often did. Her skin smelled just like I remembered it would. I wanted so badly to wrap my arms around her and give her a big hug, but the tubes prevented me from letting down my guard and embracing her as I wanted.

This experience brought about a mix of gratitude for being able to be close to her, alongside a deep sorrow for the limitations imposed on me. The conflict between wanting to protect her and yearning for an intimate connection was overwhelming, adding another layer of emotional complexity to my recovery journey.

My parents and Dale gave my daughter and me space to connect. They stepped to the back and began speaking in hushed tones about the visit, as Dale was nervous as well. They were trying to avoid medical discussions in an attempt to not cause me additional stress or anxiety. The focus was on my daughter and making the visit a joyful time despite the uncertainty and fear bleeding through us all. Something also needs to be stated about Dale's nervousness of this encounter.

My family stayed for about an hour. As the visit progressed, I became increasingly exhausted. Tolerating the speaking valve was draining and I knew I needed to rest, but I dreaded the idea of saying goodbye to her as the future remained so uncertain. They left, understanding my need for recovery.

By the time they left, I was utterly exhausted. The effort to keep up with the conversation and muster the energy to speak had taken its toll. While I appreciated their visit, I was relieved to finally be alone, allowing myself the rest I so desperately needed.

As they walked out, a wave of depression crashed over me, hitting me like a semi-truck. My heart ached deeply, and the fear that this might be the last time I ever saw my daughter and parents was overwhelming. The uncertainty and dread of what lied ahead felt suffocating, and anger bubbled up inside me at the unfairness of it all. I couldn't escape the pervasive question "Why me?" which gnawed at my soul, leaving me grappling with a profound sense of injustice and despair.

A Final Plasmapheresis Treatment

The next day, I faced another plasmapheresis treatment. Cat was back and understood my anxiety and the precarious state of my veins. The team was concerned about the possibility of needing a port if my veins didn't hold up for this much-needed final round. They found a good vein using the ultrasound, hoping it would last for the final plasmapheresis treatment.

As they brought in the machine, my anxiety skyrocketed. I felt incredibly hot and nervous. At the very moment they were beginning the procedure, Dale's long-time friend and personal trainer, Janet, came to visit. Her presence was a stark reminder of my previous life when we would go to her for personal training sessions. Now, seeing me in such a vulnerable state, I couldn't hold back my tears.

Dale got up and greeted her. Jared approached her as well, shaking hands and introducing himself. They immediately got to talking about the nature of my disease, nutrition, and ingredients in the selected carton of tube feed they were giving me, and strategies to help me get my life back again. Sensing my distress, they stepped out to give me space and to continue the conversation. Cat adjusted the fan, adding a small bunch of lavender to the room to try and calm me down in a more natural way.

This visit from Janet, though brief and difficult, was another reminder of my support network. Despite my exhaustion and the relentless physical and emotional challenges, knowing that people cared and were there for me gave me a modicum of strength to keep fighting. The visit had served as a poignant reminder of my journey, underscoring the stark contrast between my past and present, but also highlighting the unwavering support of my loved ones. This network of care and concern was my lifeline, giving me the strength to endure and the hope to keep fighting.

Cat, sensing that I may have been experiencing a reaction to the medication due to my rising body temperature, brought in ice packs and placed them between my legs and under my arms. The heat was unbearable, making me feel like I was burning up from the inside out.

The ice packs provided some relief, cooling me down enough to allow the treatment to continue. I could feel the cold seeping into my skin, a stark contrast to the feverish heat that had been plaguing me throughout the past few weeks.

Dale sat by my bedside as they administered the final plasmapheresis treatment. As usual, he was off in the corner on his phone, texting and updating family and friends. His face was a mask of focus, concentration, and worry. I knew he was reaching out to one of his clients, a distinguished doctor, asking questions and seeking medical advice.

He was also deeply entrenched in conversations with the insurance company, trying to figure out what the next steps would be regarding my discharge and where I would go. His determination was unwavering, navigating the labyrinth of medical bureaucracy to ensure that I received the best possible care once I left the ICU.

The sound of his phone typing and frequent trips out of the ICU to answer calls were a constant during my treatment, a reminder of the life and caregiver responsibilities that awaited us outside of these walls.

The entire process was draining, both physically and emotionally. The machine's steady hum, the cool breeze from the fan, and the scent of lavender filled the room. I focused on these sensations, trying to distract myself from the discomfort and anxiety.

As the treatment continued, I felt a mix of gratitude and frustration. I was grateful for the care and support I was receiving but frustrated by my helplessness and dependence on others. This final plasmapheresis treatment was a crucial step toward recovery, yet it also highlighted how far I still had to go.

Despite the discomfort and heat, the treatment was completed successfully. After it had ended, the staff disconnected me from the machines, Cat removed the ice packs, and I let out a breath I hadn't realized I was holding. As the last of the plasmapheresis treatments filtered through my system, I felt an immense sense of relief and was deeply grateful that my veins had held up.

The fear of complications had loomed large, but we had made it through. Dale squeezed my hand, his expression one of support. Although the past four treatments had not seemed to provide me with any noticeable gains and despite the hardships, we were moving forward, one step at a time.

Nearly four weeks into my stay in the ICU and following grueling work with the sprinting process, I was weaned off the ventilator that had kept me alive. The milestone was miraculous, and we felt an enormous sense of relief and hope as this was a prerequisite for being able to leave the ICU and another step on the road to recovery.

At the end of the day, Dale updated my list of accomplishments with the following new additions:

- Made blanket
- Went outside with PT
- Parents visited
- Completed plasmapheresis treatments

Recovery is a series of small gains and, as I fell asleep, I felt a sense of relief that the day's challenges were finally behind me.

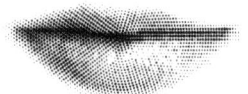

CHAPTER 8
An Emotional Departure

Tracy, my social worker, approached Dale to discuss my discharge. I was now safely extubated, meaning that I was now breathing on my own without the ventilator, however, I still had my tracheostomy tube with the trach collar, a device that attached over the end of the tube providing moisture and reducing risk of infection.

Tracy outlined our options for the next phase of recovery, which included a choice between two different Long Term Acute Care (LTAC) facilities in California: one in Riverside and the other in Perris. I would remain at one of these facilities until I had successfully completed decannulation – the process whereby the tracheostomy tube is removed, and the neck heals naturally, which could take an unknown period of time.

Dale immediately sprang into action, making phone calls and scheduling appointments to view both facilities the next day. The decision was critical; we needed a place that could provide the specialized care I required and support my ongoing recovery.

The social worker explained the amenities and care protocols of each facility, highlighting their differences. She reassured us that both facilities were reputable and equipped to handle my needs. But we knew the choice would ultimately come down to where we felt most comfortable and confident in the level of care, as well as considerations of the driving distance for Dale.

Dale's determination was unmistakable. He knew how crucial it was to find the right place for me, a facility where I would feel safe and supported. As he organized the visits, I could see the wheels turning in his mind, weighing the pros and cons of each location, thinking through every possible scenario to ensure that we would make the best decision.

As the day ended, the weight of the decision loomed over us. Moving on from the ICU was a significant step forward, but it also meant venturing into the unknown once again.

Final PT Session

My therapy sessions continued to push my limits daily in hopes of sending me to the next phase of recovery with some semblance of my previous life. In my final week at the ICU, I had a new physical therapist named Tara. She was fit, cheerful, and full of life. She had a love of yoga as well, and we immediately bonded over that connection. Feeling grateful, I was reassured by her positivity and encouragement, which mirrored Jess' approach. Tara had heard from others about my determination and motivation, and she decided to push me further, giving me tasks most had not seen performed in this setting before.

She quickly gathered my team and prepared me for my transfer from the bed. Dale, in charge of holding my head during transfers, grabbed the sides of my head so it wouldn't fall. It was still severely compromised. He held my head in place as Tara clasped my neck brace around my neck and positioned the supporting rolled towels.

On three, they had me up and into the hallway, walking, this time only requiring three people to help me. That was progress!

"Let's do some lunges and squats today!" Tara announced with an enthusiastic smile.

What? Really? With all these tubes? How? My mind raced. But I was fully prepared to do whatever she wanted me to do. I desperately wanted my life back.

We proceeded outside my ICU room and started our journey

around the nurses' station. Remembering my first session, when I only went a few feet, I far surpassed that today. I made multiple laps walking around the nurses' station, high fiving the team of nurses as I passed them in the hallways. Chin up and proud, I finally felt like I was moving mountains.

Then came time for lunges. Tara carefully positioned herself, holding my IV pole steady. I took a deep breath, placed one foot in front of the other, and slowly lowered myself down. The movement felt both exhilarating and exhausting, each inch bringing back memories of my old self. My heart rate skyrocketed to 130 beats per minute, even though my lunges were not as deep as they used to be. Still, I felt a sense of accomplishment, a glimpse of my former strength returning.

Sensing my exhaustion, Tara brought the wheelchair closer for me to sit in and monitored my heart rate until it declined. Knowing I wouldn't be satisfied if we stopped there, she suggested we push the limits further with a few squats. I watched her as she demonstrated how to do it, mesmerized by the way her body moved. She was strong and lean, everything I used to be.

A wave of devastation hit me as I realized how much my abilities had changed; just a few weeks ago, I could perform at her level. I felt a pang of envy but did everything in my power to fight back, determined to impress her with what little strength I had left. Moving slowly, I braced myself against the wall for support and began to lower my body. Each inch of descent was a battle against the exhaustion and discomfort that seemed to grip my entire being. The effort was immense, but with each squat, I felt a tiny bit of my life returning.

As I completed the final squat, I felt a rush of relief mixed with accomplishment. My legs trembled as I sat down, but there was a sense of pride in having pushed past my limits. Tara offered a few words of praise, acknowledging my efforts. Her encouragement helped me feel a renewed sense of possibility, reminding me that each small step forward was a victory on the road to recovery.

As she helped me back up from the wheelchair, the fatigue in my muscles was palpable. She carefully moved the wheelchair out of the way, making room for me to attempt a few more exercises. She walked me back to my room, helped me into my chair, and removed my neck brace. I felt a sense of relief to have the session over, but I was also proud of what I had accomplished.

Her encouragement and the sheer will to reclaim my life propelled me forward. Despite the tubes and fatigue, I felt renewed hope with each movement.

Tara's continual encouragement, radiating positivity, and determination to help me get my life back was heartwarming, though I couldn't help but compare my current accomplishments to my past physical capabilities.

I knew that what she was witnessing was the resilience of a true ICU fighter. I was grateful for her positive spirit, encouraging words, and the comforting smile she gave me whenever I felt discouraged. Her support kept my spirits up. As she walked out of the room, a wave of sadness washed over me, knowing that discharge day was on the horizon and unsure if our paths would cross again.

Spa Day

The following day, the nurses could tell that I was exhausted, not just physically but emotionally and mentally as well. The burnout was palpable. In an effort to lift my spirits, they organized a special spa day just for me.

They gently moved me into the chair, a process that required meticulous care and coordination to manage holding up my neck and the various tubes.

Once settled, two nurses came in and started to pamper me. They massaged my feet and painted my toenails a cheerful color. Another nurse brought in a makeshift salon setup – a large waste container lined with a black trash bag, with towels draped everywhere to catch the water.

One of the nurses reclined my chair and carefully washed my hair, letting the water drain into the trash bin. The sensation of having clean, brushed hair was indescribable. They even shaved my legs, leaving me feeling refreshed and somewhat more like my old self.

The entire process was a symphony of care and compassion, each nurse playing her part to make me feel human again.

My attitude shifted noticeably. For the first time in a long while, I felt genuinely happy and a sense of relief that I would recover. Dale noticed the change too, his eyes lighting up as he said, "Wow, you look happy. You look good, Vanessa."

He thanked the nursing staff profusely and I did too, my gratitude evident in my eyes and words. Those small gestures from the staff were incredibly impactful, lifting my spirits when I was in one of the darkest places of my life.

It gave me a sense of dignity and helped me reclaim a part of my lost self and identity that had been stripped from me in the ICU. For a brief moment, I felt like a human again rather than just a patient hooked up to machines. The compassion and attention to detail the nurses showed made a world of difference, restoring a small piece of my shattered spirit.

That night Dale updated my list of accomplishments with the following:

- Did squats and lunges in the hallway
- Walked around the nurses' station twice
- Spa day

Facing Uncertainty: Would I Survive without Jared?

Day by day, the discussion surrounding my discharge was becoming more frequent. "Now that she is on the trache collar and not relying on the ventilator, she can be safely downgraded to a lower level of care," the doctors told Dale.

One of my nurses had previously explained that a trache collar was a device used to deliver humidified oxygen to patients with a tracheostomy. Unlike a ventilator, which mechanically assists or controls breathing, the trache collar allowed me to breathe on my own while ensuring that I received the necessary oxygen and humidity.

Being transitioned to a trache collar was a significant milestone in my recovery, indicating that my respiratory function had improved enough to manage breathing without the constant support of a ventilator.

With each passing day on the trache collar I grew stronger, and my confidence in my ability to recover increased. The doctors and nurses closely monitored my progress, and their reports were increasingly positive. It was clear that I was making strides in my recovery.

I woke up one day feeling a sense of sadness. I tried to conceal it but had to face the inevitable. Today was Jared's final day in the ICU, the last day he would be a member of my care team. I wondered if I would survive. He came into my room that final morning, his presence a mix of familiarity and impending loss. He did his usual routine, asking both me and Dale about the previous night and how I was feeling with everything changing around me.

I spent every spare moment between therapies doing my swallow exercises, but despite my efforts, my progress seemed stagnant. I tried to focus on the positive; my physical therapy sessions were showing real improvement, which gave me a semblance of hope amidst the ongoing challenges of secretion buildup.

As the day wore on, I kept a close eye on the clock, knowing Jared would be leaving around 5:00 or 6:00 p.m. In the afternoon, he came to my room and took a seat next to me. He shared that it was his last day and, even though I had been preparing for it, I couldn't hold back my tears. I poured out my gratitude, telling him how profoundly his care had impacted me.

Dale, usually stoic, became emotional too – one of the rare moments I saw him so openly vulnerable during this ordeal. They embraced and I cried, overwhelmed by everything I felt I had lost and the uncertainty of what laid ahead. I reminded myself that I still had my medical advocate, Dale, at my side. But not having someone there now for Dale concerned me, as Jared had been his go-to person for clarification and support during the most challenging experience of our lives.

I looked at him with tears in my eyes and said, "You know, one day, I'll write a book about all this, and you'll be in it." I spoke with a hint of sarcasm but also a hopeful playfulness. "And maybe you'll even write the foreword," I added jokingly. He smiled and nodded his head, squeezing my hand warmly. "I'd like that," he replied. He left on a positive note, but my heart ached with the weight of our parting and the uncertain journey still ahead.

The next day was tough. I woke up knowing Jared wouldn't be there. He was moving on to bigger things, becoming a doctor, and I had to face the reality of my continued recovery without him.

It was a difficult transition, but I knew I had to keep moving forward. His absence was a void, a reminder of the transient nature of support in a medical setting.

Finding a Rehab Facility and Being Discharged

The next day brought new challenges. Not only was Jared no longer at the ICU, but Dale also had to visit two potential rehab facilities for me, a task that was emotionally taxing for both of us. He had to drive about an hour and a half to two hours away, leaving me to rely only on the nursing staff for support.

To pass the time while he was away, I spent every minute of unscheduled time doing my swallow exercises. Lindsey had only said to do 10-15 of each, but I was motivated and did twice that. I was also given stretch bands which I used in bed to strengthen my still immobile right arm. The continual coughing of secretions continued to be a significant challenge and didn't appear to be lessening as time went by, leaving me exhausted at the end of each day.

Dale returned with a comprehensive overview of the rehab facilities, discussing my options in great detail with me. He had visited one and gathered information about the other. He presented his findings methodically, recounting each facility's unique features and what he believed would best support my recovery journey. His descriptions included specifics about the facilities' amenities, such as private rooms, nurse-to-patient ratio, and rehabilitation (gym) facilities. He also highlighted the staff's qualifications and their approach to patient care.

I communicated with him my concern of finding a location that was also close to home, ensuring that he would be able to be present to advocate for me on a daily basis. I only felt secure having him nearby as he was the only one who knew my history and preferences. I also hoped to be able to see my parents and daughter more frequently if I were in closer proximity to where they lived.

His dedication to finding the right fit for me was all-encompassing. He had thoroughly researched each option to ensure that every detail aligned with my needs and preferences. His commitment to determining the most supportive and effective environment for me was evident, and his thorough approach gave me a sense of reassurance and hope for the next phase of my recovery.

As my time in the ICU was winding down, the reality of discharge day quickly set in. I was making progress with the speaking valve, and everything seemed to be moving toward discharge despite my slow progress on swallowing. It was clear that I would be leaving soon, and with Jared gone, I felt nervously optimistic about beginning this next phase. It felt symbolic as if, now that he was gone, it was time for me to move on as well.

Discharge Day

The day I had been waiting for had finally arrived. I woke up feeling restless as I didn't sleep well in anticipation of all the transition. The nurses were no longer giving me stronger medications to sleep, so I had to rely on Benadryl to get me through the sleepless nights, which for me wasn't enough. I reflected on the fact that Jared wouldn't be coming by to check on me. That scared me, but with each passing day things were getting somewhat easier to manage without him. Still, the sense of loss and abandonment lingered.

Alongside a certain gratifying feeling of my own "graduation" from the ICU, I experienced a low-level mix of panic and fear. I was leaving the safety and familiarity of this place, where the nurses knew me so well, and moving into the unknown.

The ICU had become a sanctuary of sorts, a place where I felt understood. Each nurse had become a friend, with shifts marked by shared moments of vulnerability and such compassionate and loving care. I felt some apprehension resurfacing about the unknowns of my new care team, their understanding of my case and specific needs, and how my pain and neck paralysis would be managed. It was a bit overwhelming to think about. I dreaded the thought of explaining my condition all over again to new faces but reminded myself that I still had Dale to advocate for me on this journey. I was not alone.

We were at a complete loss for how to properly thank my team for everything they had done. So, Dale did what he knew best – he brought in treats. He carefully selected platters of assorted cookies and muffins, which he delivered with heartfelt gratitude to the nurses' break room as a symbol of our deep appreciation. We hoped that one day, under better circumstances and with my PEG tube removed, we might have the chance to see them all again and share a bite to eat together.

Various people on my team kept meandering in and out of my room to check on us and wish us luck on the next phase. It was a nice gesture and reminded me how truly dedicated they were to their patients. I felt like our lives mattered to each and every one of them. My life had been changed by every medical professional who entered my room that month.

One memorable encounter that day was when one of the ICU doctors came in, sat down next to Dale, and answered any last-minute questions we had. The doctor looked at Dale and said with a striking honesty, "You make me want to be a better husband." For a man to be vulnerable like that was shocking to me. He saw the countless hours Dale had put in at my bedside, the questions he had been asking, and his dedication to helping the team get me well again. It was very touching.

Hearing those words, I saw a new depth of emotion in Dale's eyes. It was a rare moment where the immense strain and stress of the past weeks seemed to ease, if only for a moment. His devotion, unwavering support, and ability to stay strong through everything were being acknowledged in a profound way. He smiled.

As the doctor left, I felt a sense of deep gratitude. These medical professionals were more than just caregivers; they were compassionate individuals who had walked with us through one of the most challenging times of our lives. Their dedication and kindness had made a lasting impact, and I knew that Dale and I would carry their support with us as we moved forward into the next phase of our journey.

The EMTs arrived to take me to the rehab facility, and their professionalism was evident as they carefully moved me onto the gurney. They discussed the discharge procedures with Dale, who signed the necessary papers.

I had my speaking valve on at that moment but kept my phone nearby in case I needed another form of communication. The fear of something going wrong during the ambulance ride and not being able to communicate was intense, but I reassured myself that I had my phone for backup should the speaking valve fail.

Before we left the ICU for the last time, the charge nurse approached Dale with a grateful smile. "Thank you for being so attentive and supportive during your wife's stay," she said, her voice full of appreciation. "We don't often see caregivers as engaged and involved as you have been, and I want to express my gratitude for all the help you've given us." Dale's face softened, and he felt a wave of gratitude wash over him. "Thank you" he replied sincerely. "We couldn't have gotten through this without your dedication and compassion. You've all been so attentive to Vanessa's needs, and I'm incredibly grateful for everything you do. Your kindness and care have made a world of difference to us.

With a final remark of thanks, we turned and headed toward the exit. As I was pushed down the hallway, a mix of emotions flooded us. Relief at finally leaving the ICU after so many long, anxious days. Gratitude for the incredible care, compassion and support we had received. And an overwhelming sense of awe at the journey we had just been through. It was hard to believe we were leaving behind a place that had witnessed some of our darkest and most challenging moments, yet also where we found strength, friendship and hope. Stepping through those doors for the last time felt like stepping into a new chapter, carrying with us the lessons we had learned and the profound changes we felt within ourselves.

As they wheeled me out of my ICU room and down the hallway to the doors where I would leave the hospital, my home for so many weeks now, the halls were lined with nurses and respiratory therapists, all there to say goodbye. It was incredibly emotional. I felt like I was leaving a part of myself behind.

Each face in the hallway represented a piece of my journey, and their smiles and tears were testaments to the bond we had formed. They were not just healthcare providers; they had become part of my extended family. The ICU had been my world for so long, and the thought of leaving this cocoon of safety was both exciting and terrifying.

I didn't want to leave yet I did at the same time. I knew that to leave meant to start healing in a new way. What I really wanted was to go back to my previous life, but in the current moment, that life as I knew was over.

I glanced at Dale, who walked beside the gurney, holding my hand. His face showed a mix of pride and anxiety as we said our goodbyes. He had been my rock, and the uncertainty ahead weighed heavily on both of us.

The EMTs gently loaded me into the ambulance, securing the gurney and ensuring that I was comfortable. The doors closed and, as the engine started, I looked out the window at the hospital one last time, trying to make sense of what had unfolded over the past month. This was the first time I had been in a vehicle since my experience arriving there, when I was lying supine on a fentanyl-induced psychedelic trip. Now I was sitting upright, able to see the open road behind me. UCSD had been a place of both immense pain and healing, a paradox that I was only beginning to understand.

As the ambulance drove away, I held onto the hope that this next step to an LTAC facility would bring me closer to recovery. All I could see was the sky and the tree-lined road behind us, yet the fear of the unknown loomed large, a constant companion on this journey.

While we were turning to enter the freeway, Dale pulled up right behind us, following immediately behind the ambulance as we proceeded to the facility. I looked over at the EMT sitting next to me, pointed out the back window to Dale in the car, shrugged my shoulders, sighed, and said, "In sickness and in health." The EMT nodded, his eyes reflecting a deep understanding, and he replied with genuine warmth, "Absolutely. That's true love right there."

The ride to the LTAC facility felt like an eternity. Each bump in the road was a reminder of my fragile state. The atmosphere was quiet with nervous anticipation. The journey was far from over, but with each step I was closer to reclaiming my life.

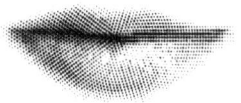

CHAPTER 9
A Journey Through Rehabilitation and Home

After my stay in the ICU at UCSD, I was transferred to an LTAC to begin my rehabilitation journey. The goal was to get me decannulated, but one rehab facility ultimately wouldn't accept me because I had a tracheostomy and required a higher level of care and was a higher risk of an adverse event. A nurse had once explained to me that decannulation involved the removal of my trache and the closure of my stoma, emphasizing what a significant and critical step this was in my recovery.

When the ambulance took me from UCSD to the LTAC, I was not on a ventilator but had a trache collar. During the ride, I remembered feeling the emotional toll as I looked out the back window and saw my husband's car trailing behind the ambulance. The vows of "in sickness and in health" took on a new depth.

Dale wouldn't leave my side, even following the ambulance to ensure that I got there safely. The sight of his car was both a comfort and a reminder of how much our lives had changed. It was a surreal moment, lying there, feeling the movement of the ambulance, and seeing the familiar car that symbolized stability and love amidst the chaos.

Arriving at the LTAC, I was greeted by the unexpected sight of my parents and daughter as they pulled my gurney out of the back end of the ambulance. While it was heartwarming for them to greet us like this, I felt a deep sense of embarrassment. Although I was sitting up, I didn't want my daughter to remember me being wheeled out of an ambulance. I wanted to hold her, but I knew now wasn't the time.

As they pushed me through the LTAC, the contrast with UCSD was stark.

The walls were filthy, covered in layers of dirt and grime, and the floors were scuffed and worn. The entire building appeared old and neglected, with peeling paint and flickering fluorescent lights. The air was thick with the smell of antiseptic mixed with something stale and musty. The noise from patient monitors and alarms added to the unwelcoming feeling.

It was nothing like the freshly painted, modern, and sterile environment at UCSD. My heart sank as I realized this was where I would have to fight my next battles.

Dale hid his worries well, but I could sense his concern as he surveyed the environment. This was one hospital he hadn't been able to observe beforehand, but he decided to send me here because it supposedly had good reviews and was closer to home.

I had been told I would have a roommate but, upon arrival, my room was empty. The EMTs transferred me from the gurney to my bed, and the moment I settled into it, I felt how uncomfortable it was. The mattress was soft and depleted of any cushion, worn down from years of use by countless previous patients. It sagged in the middle, and I quickly sank into the crack, feeling the lack of support on my back. The sheets were thin and scratchy, adding to my discomfort. The bed creaked with every slight movement, a constant reminder of how old and worn it was.

The room was hot, but considering I was always hot at the previous hospital, I initially dismissed it. Dale, feeling the heat too, took off his sweater and asked if the air conditioning was on. The nurse responded, "Yes," but we later learned from a repairman who arrived a few hours later that it had been broken for several days. It felt like we were being lied to already in the first hour, heightening our anxiety and adding to our growing list of concerns.

Dale immediately got to work putting up the pictures from my previous wall on the new, albeit strikingly dirty, wall in front of me in an attempt to keep my motivation going. This new staff wasn't nearly as intrigued by the pictures as my previous team, solidifying in my mind that this was just a job for them and that I was just another patient. The lack of interest in my personal touches felt like another layer of detachment, making me feel even more isolated and unimportant in this new environment.

The red flags were glaring. For one, children weren't allowed inside, so they told me I had to see my daughter through a dirty, water-stained window. The sight of her on the other side, unable to come in and hug me, broke my heart and amplified my anxiety, as all I wanted to do was snuggle up with her now that I did not have as many tubes strapped to me. Upon learning about this protocol, my parents packed up my daughter and left the hospital. I was looking forward to holding her in my arms again, and felt stripped of that connection I so desperately needed.

The next red flag was the indifferent attitude of the nurse, who didn't even acknowledge my attempts at small talk or make any eye contact as I tried to make a joke to lighten the mood. She just sat at her computer, typing away. Dale and I shared a look of concern, realizing that this wasn't the level of care we were used to.

The final red flag was the requirement for family members to vacate the building after eight hours. Why? What was happening behind closed doors that they didn't want us to see? Dale was my advocate, and his absence filled me with fear. The thought of being left alone in such an impersonal and uncaring environment was terrifying.

Before leaving that night, Dale meticulously reviewed with the night nurse the medications I was on and how to properly care for my PEG tube and feed me. To our dismay, they had the medications incorrect – some dosages were wrong, and others were entirely missing from the list. Their lack of familiarity with my tube and how to feed me had us both on edge.

Thankfully, UCSD provided us with enough of the organic tube feed to last the month, which we kindly offered to the new staff. As expected, they were unsure of what to do with it, as they had never seen anything organic before. Once again, Dale was there to teach them, ensuring that they understood how to handle and administer it properly.

He was hesitant to leave me that first night, given all that had unfolded during the day. I could see the reluctance and worry in his eyes. He double-checked everything, making sure I had my phone and charger and knew how to use it if needed. He also made sure my call button was within reach, remembering the late-night call he got from me at UCSD.

When he finally had to leave, he leaned in close and whispered that he would be back as soon as they allowed him in. It was a terrifying prospect for both of us – being left alone in a place where I already felt so vulnerable and where the care seemed so poor.

I clung to my phone like a lifeline, knowing it was my only way to reach out for help.

I woke up in the middle of the night, struggling to breathe due to a buildup of secretions. I hit the call button. I hit it again and again, panic rising with each passing second. After what felt like an eternity of wondering whether I might die, a nurse finally arrived to help me with suctioning.

The 20-minute wait had been agonizing, leaving me shaken and deeply worried about the level of care I was receiving and concerned that the lack of care might kill me.

I spent the night slipping down in bed and needing assistance to reposition, but help was slow to come. The anxiety of not being able to move myself and the discomfort of slipping into the crack of the bed made sleep elusive.

I laid awake, staring at the ceiling, my mind filled with fears and frustrations. The staff was unprofessional, turning on lights and talking loudly whenever they entered my room. I desperately needed rest to heal, but it was impossible with their constant interruptions.

I woke up the next day in a rage at the lack of care I had received during the night. When Dale returned, he immediately complained to management about the poor service.

The staff assured us that changes would be made, but their words felt hollow, like a rehearsed script meant to placate us. It was clear they were overwhelmed. The nurses rushed between patients, their exhaustion evident, and each promise of improvement sounded more like an attempt to silence us than a genuine commitment to better care.

Every interaction left me frustrated. Were they truly aware of our distress, or were we just another complaint to manage? It felt like we were being brushed aside, navigating our loved one's care in a system stretched far too thin.

That afternoon, they brought a new patient into my room. I knew she was on a ventilator by the repetitive thumping of the machine next to me. She was completely sedated and nonresponsive. Dale, recognizing the sounds of her struggling to breathe, told the nurse she needed suctioning. The nurse dismissed his concern and quickly left the room. In complete shock, Dale immediately informed her family member when he came to visit, giving them the opportunity to speak up.

I quickly realized I was likely the only patient who was not fully sedated, and I was cognitively aware of my surroundings. Most were sadly in a declining state, their beds surrounded by the hum of ventilators and the beep of monitors. The other patients were completely unresponsive, heavily sedated, and lost in their own worlds.

This facility felt like a last resort for many, a place where hope seemed to have been almost abandoned. Wheelchairs lined the hallways, some occupied by patients who stared blankly ahead, others occupied by those who seemed to be asleep or unconscious.

The nurses moved methodically, their faces showing signs of fatigue and detachment, reinforcing the sense that I didn't belong here. My awareness and relative mobility made me feel out of place, highlighting the stark contrast between my condition and that of the other patients. This realization was isolating and unsettling, amplifying my anxiety and reinforcing the notion that I was in a facility not equipped to handle someone with my potential for recovery.

After Dale and I spent the day together—eight hours, to be precise—an announcement over the intercom instructed all visitors to leave the building because Visiting Hours had ended. Everyone was to leave except patients. We were prisoners. Reluctantly, Dale gathered his belongings and prepared to leave, glancing back at me with worry. As the door closed behind him, a wave of panic washed over me at the thought of being alone again. I felt a tightening in my chest, knowing he had to go. I hoped nothing would happen while he was away, but a chilling sense of dread settled in as I realized that if something did occur, the staff would likely do nothing to help me.

Once outside, he found a spot in the parking lot and sat in his car to eat dinner, the solitude amplifying his anxiety and concern. I wished I had a way to relieve both of our worries and anxieties about the future, but instead, I was left with the solitude of my room and the sounds of machines around me. I couldn't help but think about what was next—what if this was my forever? Images of my daughter flooded my mind, amplifying my loneliness and grief as I longed for my previous life.

A Toileting Nightmare

As days passed, I progressed from having to use the awkward and uncomfortable bedpan to now using a bedside commode, though I still required nursing assistance for the transfer due to the neck brace needed for this challenging task.

All alone in the room, I pushed the call button but, as expected, no one came. I pressed it again and waited for a minute. Frustrated, I began hitting it repeatedly, hoping the continuous ringing would catch the nurses' attention. I realized that if this were a true medical emergency, I could have been in serious trouble, but thankfully it wasn't.

In frustration, I called out, "I need to go to the bathroom!" The nurse entered my room. Clearly impatient herself, she grabbed my neck brace and put it on, preparing me for the transfer. She placed me on the commode and then left.

After I finished using the commode, I realized I needed help returning to bed. Unfortunately, my call button was left on my bed, just three feet away from me, out of my reach. I should have known they would carelessly overlook this important piece of my care. Despite knowing that I shouldn't stand up, I had no choice but to try and reach the call button myself. The frustration mounted as I weighed the risk against my urgent need for assistance. I stood up, carefully shuffling my feet toward the bed. I grabbed the remote and forcefully pressed the call button, but no one came. I pressed it again, still no response. I glanced at the clock, noting the time as each minute ticked by. I sat on the commode for a grueling 25 minutes before someone finally arrived to help me.

When Dale returned and heard about the ordeal of being left alone without any help, he immediately took action, notifying management about this unacceptable situation. As usual, management offered apologies and empty promises, but nothing changed. Their continual lies only deepened our frustration and mistrust.

I reminded myself that the goal was to become decannulated here and then I could leave. We became hyper-focused on the decannulation process in hopes of leaving soon. Dale, my advocate, kept asking when this procedure would take place, and given the environment, I was highly motivated to proceed.

That night before leaving, Dale had to teach the new nurse how to use my PEG tube for feeding and medication, once again. They never seemed to have the same nurse back-to-back as I had grown accustomed to. This added to my anxiety and sense of vulnerability.

The thought of relying on people who didn't know how to care for me properly was horrifying. He also had to instruct the new team how I still needed the towel rolls on my pillow and why I needed them placed the way I did, but to no avail.

I endured another sleepless night as medical personnel frequently entered my room for late-night cleanings, emptying trash cans, and sweeping the floors. I was frustrated, questioning why these tasks couldn't be done during the day. Each new person who entered turned on the lights, and I could overhear conversations from the hallway, adding to my irritation.

Overwhelmed, I shouted at one of the staff members, demanding that they be quiet, turn off the lights, and not come back.

Still, later on, and in the middle of the night, a figure in a white coat entered my room, attempting to collect blood samples. He struggled, repeatedly failing to draw blood. I told him my veins were severely damaged and filled with scar tissue from the previous hospital stays, making it nearly impossible to get a sample without an ultrasound machine.

Frustrated and exhausted, I instructed him to stop trying and leave. My patience was wearing thin with the continuous challenges and the staff's apparent lack of understanding and compassion. Before leaving, he said he would get a referral for an ultrasound machine and come back tomorrow.

The next morning, I was rudely awakened by my occupational therapist yelling my name from the hallway. It felt like the abuse would never end. "Vanessa, get up and get dressed – it's time for therapy!" What happened to a nice and gentle "Good morning? How are you feeling?" Or "How was your night" or even an introduction before jumping right into therapy? What happened to the humanistic side of the medical world? It was gone as I knew it at this place.

I wanted to get well and participate, so I tried to brush off her rudeness and move forward, but I was disappointed. I worked my way through the session, but neither one of us talked very much. After the session, she assured me that if I wanted to get out of bed and have extra time to walk the halls, I should just hit the call button, and someone would come to assist me. Unfortunately, it never worked as promised.

After numerous calls and Dale repeatedly asking the staff, help finally arrived after significant delays. I even went so far as to take the heart rate and pulse oximeter off my body to see whether that would cause the staff to respond in a timelier manner, but it didn't do a thing. This constant struggle to get the assistance I needed was deeply concerning.

I saw the speech therapist only twice during my time there. When Dale, my medical advocate, inquired about this, the response was that she was part-time. Despite our requests for more frequent visits, we were denied without a clear explanation, leaving me in a state of confusion and frustration, especially since I remained designated NPO and received all of my intake via my feeding tube. Because I only saw her twice, there was no opportunity to really create any meaningful target goals. I wondered what she even wrote in my evaluation.

As a speech-language pathologist myself, I remained committed to the swallowing exercises provided by my previous SLP, determined to continue strengthening myself despite the limited support. If good-quality skilled intervention was not going to be provided to me, I would continue to work on my swallowing exercises independently.

Dale's constant advocacy often led to confrontations with staff, who were defensive and dismissive of his concerns. It was clear that they didn't appreciate his questions or his insistence on proper care. We felt like we were fighting a losing battle, trying to get the care I needed in a place that seemed indifferent to my suffering.

Waiting and Waiting

I had been there for two days, and the one person I desperately needed to see had yet to appear. The respiratory therapist was critical to starting the decannulation process, a crucial step in my recovery.

I knew that decannulation and capping trials were pivotal steps in needed to take as part of the removal of my tracheostomy tube. These steps required a respiratory therapist to carefully manage the overall process to ensure that I could breathe, swallow, and clear secretions safely and effectively, regaining normal breathing and voicing. There were some things I could do on my own with regard to therapy, but this was not one of them.

Without the respiratory therapist's expertise, I was stuck, unable to advance to the next phase of breathing on my own. His absence was causing a significant delay in my progress and increasing my anxiety about the path ahead.

I was, however, using the speaking valve for communication and had managed to keep it on during all my waking hours. One evening, I reached a point where I urgently needed it removed due to fatigue. The nurse, seemingly misunderstanding my request, tightened it even further.

Dale watched in growing frustration as the nurse struggled with it, and eventually, he had to step in. Despite his efforts to loosen it, he couldn't get it off, and panic began to set in as I struggled to breathe.

Feeling desperate, Dale rushed to the nursing station, demanding that someone come immediately to correct the situation. After what felt like an excruciatingly long wait, another team member finally arrived and managed to remove the valve. Exhausted and on edge, I glanced at Dale with a look of shock and disbelief, silently conveying my need to escape this place.

I sat in bed, tears streaming down my face. I was overwhelmed by fear, loneliness, and sheer exhaustion from the relentless stress of being in this place. Every day felt like an uphill battle, and I was emotionally and physically drained.

Dale, deeply concerned and hesitant to leave me in the hands of yet another unfamiliar nurse, decided to take matters into his own hands regarding my nightly tube feeding. He carefully administered my tube feeding himself before heading home that night. While I was grateful for his support, I couldn't help but feel a mix of comfort and embarrassment, knowing that he had to step in to ensure that I received the care I desperately needed.

In the wee hours of the morning, I woke up in a panic and needed suctioning. Miraculously, a respiratory therapist came in within a reasonable amount of time, and I was pleasantly shocked. She was young and articulate, and she offered reassurance that no one else here had previously offered. I was grateful and felt I finally had one staff member on my side.

As the nursing and cleaning staff continued their relentless routine of waking up every patient with their round-the-clock cleanings and wellness checks, I finally reached my breaking point. I propped myself up in bed and shouted with fury for everyone on my team to come to my room. Desperate for relief, I also called for the kind respiratory therapist, the only person who seemed to understand my needs.

When they gathered at the end of my bed, I let my frustration pour out. "I have been through hell!" I cried out. "You have no idea how utterly exhausted I am, and you are preventing me from healing!" I pointed accusingly at the nurses and the cleaning lady. "You three need to take lessons from her," I said, gesturing to the respiratory therapist. "She gets it! She understands what I need!" I concluded with a firm demand, "Now leave my room and don't come back unless I call you!"

They all left, leaving behind the respiratory therapist, who stared at me in stunned silence. Feeling both relieved and vulnerable, I laid back and let my tears flow. The respiratory therapist, sensing my distress, took out her phone and showed me a video. It was a video of the respiratory therapist who would be coming in the next day to start the decannulation process. The video highlighted his expertise and impressive reputation. Seeing this brought me a profound sense of relief, and I was deeply grateful for her kindness and for taking the time to reassure me. This surge of emotion depleted all my remaining energy, and I quickly fell back asleep.

A few hours later, I was jolted awake again by the same person from the night before, insisting on taking another blood sample. I reminded him of my damaged veins and firmly told him not to attempt it again without an ultrasound machine. Remembering his earlier promise that he would have one today, I called him a "rat" for lying and demanded that he leave me alone, regardless of the reason for the blood draw. I was done with the endless disruptions and the lack of respect for my condition.

When I woke up, I was feeling a spark of optimism and eagerness for the day ahead, particularly because the respiratory therapist was scheduled to come in. Despite sharing my frustrations and disappointments with Dale about the night before, I couldn't wait to update him about the promising news regarding the decannulation process.

A Nerve-wracking Decannulation

True to what was promised the previous day, the respiratory therapist and medical team entered my room to begin the decannulation process. I was equally filled with anticipation and anxiety.

Lying in my bed, I could feel my heart pounding as they prepared for the procedure. The respiratory therapist explained each step to me, ensuring that I understood what was about to happen. He began by monitoring my vital signs closely, making sure that my respiratory status was stable. Because of the previous lack of professionalism, poor communication, and lack of skilled nursing staff, my anxiety began to spike.

As the moment approached, the respiratory therapist carefully removed the dressing around my tracheostomy site. I took a deep breath, trying to remain as still as possible. With steady hands, the doctor slowly and gently withdrew the tracheostomy tube from my neck.

There was a brief, uncomfortable sensation, followed by a strange feeling of emptiness where the tube had been. Immediately, the nurse applied a sterile dressing over the stoma to keep it clean and aid in healing. They reassured me that everything was going smoothly and encouraged me to take deep, steady breaths.

I knew the next few hours were crucial. The medical team kept a loose watch over me, and I couldn't shake the feelings of distrust. They were supposed to ensure that my breathing remained steady and that I didn't experience any respiratory distress, but their casual demeanor made me uneasy.

They gave me clear instructions to alert them immediately if I felt short of breath or had any difficulties, yet I worried whether they'd respond quickly enough if I actually did. As I laid there, the reality of breathing on my own without the tracheostomy tube began to sink in. It was a significant and emotional step forward in my recovery, but the lack of trust in my care team added a layer of anxiety to this critical moment.

A Tough Decision

Physical therapy sessions continued but not as often as I truly needed. The therapist got me out of bed and strapped into my neck brace. He had me do a few heel raises followed by walking in place. I couldn't help thinking what a waste of time these exercises were because those areas of my body were completely unaffected by the disease.

Frustrated and with a slight attitude, I asked to go walk outside because the current exercises were "too easy." "Rome wasn't built in a day," he said, indicating that recovery takes time and is a process. Eventually, he caved and we proceeded outside. I went around the building and even climbed a few stairs, a small victory that took immense effort. The fresh air and sunlight were a welcome change from the dirty hospital environment. It felt like a tiny step toward normalcy, even though it was exhausting and required all my strength.

Now that I was decannulated and ready to intensify my rehabilitation, heated dialogues erupted between Dale and the social worker. I was eager to push harder and achieve more milestones, but it seemed there were always excuses from the therapists, which prevented them from matching my drive for progress and recovery.

Dale, trying to maintain his composure, asked about the next phase of my recovery on a daily basis. The social worker would respond to his request by saying, "We are waiting for the paperwork," and in frustration, he would walk out.

It was clear that Dale had to visit rehab facilities to find a suitable place for my next stage of recovery. This was a tough decision for him as he didn't want to leave me alone at the facility. My mother stayed with me that day, doing her best to comfort me while Dale was gone. She brushed my hair, her fingers gently working through the knots, and brought adult coloring books to try to lift my spirits.

Dale left to begin the difficult process of finding a new place for the next stage of my recovery, which meant leaving me alone. The thought of being separated from him made my stomach twist. I knew it was necessary, but the idea of facing those walls without his reassuring presence was daunting.

My mother's presence was comforting, but it didn't erase the fear gnawing at me. As the minutes ticked by, I wondered what Dale was doing—if he was finding places that felt right or if he was just as anxious as I was. Dale returned with a couple of options, and we faced a heart-wrenching decision: whether to opt for a high-end rehab facility far from home called Casa Colina or for Desert Regional, a local hospital where I could see my daughter every day.

Casa Colina was known as a very high-end and state-of-the-art rehabilitation facility in Southern California. It was considered the "elite" of all facilities, a place where everyone went for severe brain injuries, concussions, strokes, etc. It had a reputation for being new, clean, and luxurious. The sound of it was enticing after my time at the LTAC. I was hopeful. Maybe they would be able to diagnose and fix me.

The local hospital had a good reputation, was local and close to home, offering me the opportunity to heal my broken heart and see my daughter more regularly. We mulled over this agonizing decision, debating the pros and cons. I wanted the best, but I also desperately needed time with my daughter, whom I missed more than my previous self.

God works in mysterious ways and that day a neurologist came into my room. My mom and I, unsure about where to go or what to do next, asked him for his advice. Without hesitation, he advised us to choose the local facility, emphasizing the importance of family in the healing process. His words struck a profound chord with me. Healing wasn't just about physical recovery – it was about the emotional comfort and support provided by being close to loved ones.

With tears in my eyes and a heavy heart, we decided to go back to my hometown for the final stop on my medical journey. It was a difficult choice, as I felt torn between top-level care and my need to be with family, but it was the right decision by far. The thought of being surrounded by my family, feeling their support, and drawing strength from their presence felt crucial to my recovery.

I later realized that my body just needed time to heal and that a different approach would not have made a difference, as the nerves simply needed time to regenerate, and even the best staff in the world couldn't fast-forward that process.

A good friend and colleague of mine, Ashley, worked diligently behind the scenes at Desert Regional Medical Center, where she worked as a PRN, a sort of on-call nurse, ensuring that everything was ready and in order for my arrival. Knowing that someone we trusted was looking out for me made a huge difference. Her support was a beacon of hope in an otherwise difficult time.

Finally, the day came for me to be transferred to my hometown and my final rehab facility.

The discharge from the LTAC was delayed due to paperwork issues, which only added to our frustration. However, despite these challenges, there were moments of relief and support that helped us persevere. No one lined the halls or waved to us as we left the building. That was a sign to me that I was simply a medical number to them, nothing more. They made their money off me, and I was, without a doubt, ready to move on.

Final Rehab Setting

When I arrived at Desert Regional Medical Center, the contrast was immediately evident. The walls were immaculate, and the floors gleamed with polish, a welcome sign of cleanliness. The nurse who greeted us was warm and upbeat, her positive demeanor a comforting change from the previous facility.

My room was spacious and pristine, a stark contrast to the dilapidated environment I had just left. I even had a private bathroom, which felt like a luxury. The air conditioning worked perfectly, providing a refreshing escape from the oppressive heat of the old place.

This clean, well-maintained environment instilled a renewed sense of hope in me. I felt that Desert Regional Medical Center might truly be the place where I could begin to recover and rebuild. As we talked, Dale got to work wallpapering my room again with my pictures of my daughter. I was immediately starting to feel more at ease.

This new setting demanded that I actively participate in daily therapy, which I had the stamina and motivation to do. However, therapy required me to be dressed, and the all-day hospital gown was no longer acceptable. Dale brought me some gym clothes from home, but we quickly discovered that my previous wardrobe no longer fit due to my significant weight loss and inability to lift my arms. To address this, we opted for oversized V-neck shirts and cardigans, which made dressing easier and more manageable given my current limitations.

I woke up the first morning eager to begin an intense regimen of therapy. My nurse came in to give me my morning tube feed and get me dressed for the day. My occupational therapist entered my room next, welcomed me to the facility, and introduced herself. Sarah was young with long, blonde hair, and informed me that part of my OT would involve taking a shower. I had never anticipated being asked to do this, especially with my PEG tube in place. I was stunned and struggled to hide my shock and anxiety. It had been over a month since my last shower, and the thought of exposing myself in this state was overwhelming.

Reluctantly, I got out of bed and shuffled into my private shower. Too shocked to even cry, I sat on a plastic shower chair as she helped me undress piece by piece. She might have done this numerous times as an occupational therapist, but I was truly embarrassed; this was the first time I had showered in front of someone other than my husband. She was all business as she handed me the shower wand to hold with my one functioning left arm and the soap to lather up my body.

As Sarah turned on the water, I experienced a confusing mix of relief and embarrassment. The hot water felt incredible against my skin, but seeing my frail, skinny body for the first time was shocking. I held a plastic bag over my PEG tube while she washed my hair. My long, unkempt hair fell out in large clumps, clogging the drain – a humbling and emotional moment.

The experience left me feeling despondent, realizing that this daily routine would be a constant reminder of how much I had changed and how much I still had to endure.

Physical Therapy Ends, Speech Therapy Continues

I continued to struggle with daily speech therapy, making no progress despite my efforts. My speech therapist assigned new swallowing exercises, including something called chin tucks which I did religiously. I felt silly doing them because all it felt like I was doing was putting a rolled-up towel under my chin and then forcibly "tucking my chin" into that towel about 10 times. As expected, I didn't feel I made any improvement, and I felt these exercises were a waste of time.

The secretions were still problematic, and I was also developing vocal cord stridor. These are horrible, high-pitched, wheezing sounds caused by vocal cord paresis, which sadly were brought on by nerve damage to my neck area. They caused breathing difficulties, and I hated them. They were terribly scary and often made me wonder if they would cost me my life as I sat there wheezing, unable to get air into my lungs.

After one week, we anticipated that since my progress with mobility and independence had increased, I would be discharged home. But my insurance approved an additional week, per the recommendations of the therapy team. This extension left me feeling that I was still medically fragile, which was disheartening.

I was eager to go home, but also aware that Dale wasn't fully prepared for my return. Being a caregiver would be a challenge he likely wasn't prepared to face. Perhaps the persistent secretions and stridors I experienced contributed to their reluctance to discharge me home.

At the end of the first week, however, I was discharged from PT and given an extra hour of speech therapy instead. This decision frustrated me deeply, as my right arm remained immobile and I felt I still needed physical therapy.

The staff believed that OT could handle all of my physical needs, but replacing PT with more speech therapy seemed counterproductive, especially since I was fully prepared and equipped to do all the swallow exercises on my own. Despite my reservations, I had no choice but to follow their instructions, though I still felt somewhat sidelined in my recovery process.

Returning to my hometown for the final stage of my recovery provided a comforting sense of familiarity, given how the speech therapy community was very interconnected. Many of my school-based colleagues worked part-time at the hospital, so it wasn't entirely surprising when one of them appeared to give me speech therapy.

Terri was one of these colleagues and always had a positive and uplifting personality. I felt that she genuinely cared about me not only as a patient but a friend. It was comforting to be in the presence of a familiar face again. I was sad when our session together ended as she helped calm my anxiety as we discussed topics other than rehabilitation that brought a much-needed smile back to my face. It felt surreal to sit across from her, discussing voice and swallowing exercises, especially since just a few months ago, we had been discussing Individual Education Plans and school-based therapy topics.

While I no longer required the neck brace and had stopped wearing it, the staff still wanted me to wear it for additional support during therapy sessions. This small victory was a glimmer of hope in an otherwise challenging journey. But the suctioning continued to be problematic and I wasn't comfortable having my portable suction device out of reach.

Despite the progress in my ability to walk longer distances, my right arm remained paralyzed, and my swallowing exercises showed no improvement. This lack of progress was disheartening and added to my frustration and depression. Each day felt like a battle, and I often questioned whether I would ever fully recover.

Small Moments of Tranquility and Connecting

To break up the day between therapies, Dale and I would sit outside, reflecting on everything that had happened. We often sat in an awkward silence, both lost in our thoughts about the future and the uncertainty we faced. Depression was setting in more and more for me with each breath. The fresh air brought a sense of peace, even if only momentarily.

I looked forward to the afternoons when therapy ended, and my daughter could come visit. Each day, my parents would bring her after preschool, and we'd spend an hour together, catching up on her day and sharing stories. I'd prop myself up in bed, and she would snuggle close, her small hand resting on mine. We'd talk about her favorite parts of the day, and I'd listen intently, trying to stay engaged despite my fatigue.

Sometimes, we'd walk outside and I would watch her as she explored the grounds. These times together helped me feel more connected to her as her mother and made the days in the hospital a little brighter. She'd occasionally point to the large square bandage over my trache wound, her curiosity evident, and I'd gently explain it to her in a way she could understand.

On the days she was unable to come, my parents would send me videos and pictures of her at home with them baking, doing arts and crafts or her working diligently on projects with my dad around the house. It warmed my heart and reminded me how blessed I was to have their love and dedication to my child during my time of need.

In the evenings, I would often join others and sit outside on the patio, taking in the evening sunsets. The weather was nice and there was a gentle breeze calming my frazzled nerves. It was here that I met other patients, some recovering from strokes, car accidents, and brain injuries. Everyone had a different story to tell. Sharing our stories and frustrations was therapeutic. We all faced different challenges, but there was a sense of camaraderie and support among us. It was comforting to know that I wasn't alone in my struggles. This was a vivid reminder for me that my peer group was now changing, and these people were now my village.

My friends were reaching out to Dale on a consistent basis, asking questions and wondering how they could help. It felt comforting to know that once we left this place we would be surrounded by support and, hopefully, Dale would be given the opportunity to escape the new insanity that was now our life.

The stress I was under was insurmountable and the grieving process was hitting hard. In an attempt to alleviate some of that burden,

Dale found a massage therapist who was willing to come to my room and give me a chair massage. We had to lie to the staff about who she was and the purpose of her visit, but the massage was such a welcome treat and I was grateful no one stopped her.

Mother's Day came and I looked forward to spending time with my mom, although I had an ache in my heart that I was unable to do anything special for my own mother that day. I was simply grateful to spend the time with her and my daughter, knowing I very well could have been dead.

I had been at Desert Regional Medical Center for two weeks now, and I was mentally prepared to go home. I was still receiving tube feedings for all my nutritional needs and not eating or drinking anything orally. There were no significant gains in the mobility or strength of my arm, but I knew going home was where the ultimate healing would happen.

Going Home

The day finally arrived and the discharge paperwork along with it. We signed everything that needed signing, and my nurse walked us to the door. We were ready to face the next chapter together, hoping for a return to some semblance of normalcy.

It was equally exciting and terrifying. The safety and familiarity of the hospital setting was gone, and I was now stepping into a new phase of recovery. I knew that leaving the hospital didn't mean the end of my challenges; it was just a transition to facing them in a different environment.

Dale helped me into the car, making sure the neck brace was snug and secure. As we drove home, a mix of relief and fear filled the air. He drove slowly and carefully, knowing how delicate my condition was. The weight of the past few months felt heavy, but there was also a ray of hope. We were finally heading home.

While returning home was a huge milestone, it also brought new challenges. The journey through the LTAC and rehab had been tough, both physically and emotionally. The thought of adjusting to daily life, managing my ongoing medical needs, and continuing my recovery without constant medical support was overwhelming. Yet being home meant being closer to my daughter, and that gave me the strength to keep going.

As we pulled into the driveway, I looked at our house with mixed emotions. It was a symbol of the normalcy and routine I had been longing for, yet it also represented the uncertain future ahead. But for Dale, with each new chapter in my recovery, a new question seemed to surface, each one heavier than the last. "What if something happens once we're home? Will I be able to manage everything on my own? What if Vanessa doesn't improve? How will our lives change?" He wondered about the unknown, the uncertainty of their future looming like a shadow.

Dale mentioned fears of taking care of me and wondered if he could manage my complex needs with feeding. He expressed worries of leaving me home alone, making sure I had rides lined up, transportation for my daughter to and from school, food in the fridge, and activities to occupy my time. He was concerned but knew he had to go back to work in the fall. He was stuck between a rock and a hard place. There was still so much recovery ahead of us.

I had thoughts of the mounting medical bills. "How much will all this cost us? Will we be able to afford the care if I have needs in the long run?" How would we manage? Would I continue to improve? These questions filled my mind as Dale helped me out of the car and into our home.

My parents had some of the same doubts. They were incredibly worried, yet fully committed to doing whatever it took to support my rest and recovery. Much like Dale, they immediately shifted into problem-solving mode, asking, "What can we do? Do you need groceries?" Though they struggled to find the right words, their actions were guided by a deep sense of gratitude that I had survived, mixed with fear and uncertainty about what the future of my recovery would look like. They took over daily responsibilities, like taking my daughter to school and picking her up, and kept the family updated on my progress, as I was unable to communicate as often as everyone would have liked.

All of us having such overwhelming questions of doubts and feelings of inadequacies in this new area of recovery. How would we make our way through all this? One thing was certain, we would do it together.

My parents greeted me at the door, having just dropped my daughter off at preschool. It was my first time back in the house after two months, when my medical trauma began.

One thing I hadn't counted on, however, was that I wasn't the same person I was when I left — I felt fundamentally transformed, grieving the loss of my old self. While I was surrounded by the unwavering support of my parents and husband, who stood by me through every step, I couldn't shake the feeling that a part of me was missing, a part that was lost in the haze of this journey. Despite their love and reassurance, I felt like a stranger in my own body, grappling with the reality that my former self might never fully return.

A Deep Sense of Discomfort

I felt a deep sense of discomfort. The familiar surroundings now seemed foreign, and I felt like I no longer belonged. As I walked in and saw our home as it once was, I collapsed against the table, overwhelmed by the stark realization of how much had changed.

The house felt eerily empty without my daughter's presence. I longed for the life I had before, but it was painfully clear that things had changed. I spent the rest of the day sitting outside on a chair, the breeze on my face, staring at the trees for hours until she came home. I told my parents that it felt like I had just come home from my own personal war. The trauma I had experienced had been devastating, and I had so much to process. I didn't want to do anything; I had no desire to move or engage in any activity. All I could do was sit outside and reflect on everything that had happened.

My parents left, returning an hour later with my daughter. Seeing her beautiful face and big blue eyes reminded me of why I had to keep fighting. The journey was far from over, but being home, surrounded by my family, gave me the hope and determination to face whatever laid ahead.

And so, as I lied in my own bed that first night back home, I allowed myself to dream of the future – a future where I would regain my strength, return to my work, and be the mother and wife my family needed. It was a long road ahead, but I was ready to travel it, with hope in my heart and determination in my soul. The road ahead was uncertain, but I was no longer facing it alone.

First Morning Home

The next morning, I started a new walking routine before the heat became unbearable, even for desert rats. I lived on a cul-de-sac, where I walked back and forth, gradually increasing my laps every two days. With Dale and my family by my side, I felt ready to tackle the next phase of my recovery. Once it became too hot, I migrated to walking at the nearby mall in the early morning hours before shoppers arrived.

As I settled into my home routine, I realized that this journey had changed me profoundly. It had tested my limits, pushed me to my breaking point, and forced me to find strength I didn't know I had.

In addition to the physical challenges, I faced significant mental health struggles. The mental battles were intense, with thoughts of ending my life creeping into my mind. Mornings were particularly hard, and I found myself counting down the hours until nap time when I could escape into sleep and temporarily forget my pain. Napping with my daughter became a cherished ritual, offering me a brief respite from the relentless march of time and the weight of my thoughts.

It was during these times that I especially tried to focus on gratitude. One day while we were drifting off to sleep, I asked my daughter what she is grateful for and she said, "I'm grateful you're home, mommy." I cried, hugged her and replied, "So am I, honey." and we drifted off to sleep.

Every afternoon, as the mail arrived, Dale would bring it to me. My mailbox was stuffed with cards from people all over the United States who were praying for me – my "prayer warriors." Dale's mother was well connected with various church communities and sent out an email and it spread like wildfire and people all over the US started sending cards and texting me. Vanessa's Village became the name of this critical call to action. From the mustard seed of my mother-in-law's support and concern came a much-needed blessing. She continually sent emails to everyone with daily or weekly updates on how I was doing, allowing them to offer support through prayers, cards, emails, and texts.

Each connection truly felt like gifts to me and I was astonished by this outpouring of love and support. Each day, these cards lifted me up beyond words. Reading their stories of personal struggles and triumphs reminded me that I wasn't alone and that others were facing their own battles. I can't even begin to describe how many times their stories of triumph helped me stay strong and gave me the courage to keep going.

While I focused on healing, Dale immediately focused on dealing with insurance and securing the medical supplies I needed. His days were filled with phone calls and paperwork, ensuring that I had everything from tube feeding supplies to a commode, portable suction device, and shower chair.

The insurance battles were challenging, particularly over the tube-feeding formula. The one that didn't make me sick wasn't covered, forcing us to pay out of pocket. Dale's dedication was unwavering, but the stress for both of us was visible.

Insurance eventually provided all the necessary equipment, including a portable suction device, which became essential for managing my secretions. However, nowhere in my medical journey did anyone even mention, much less prepare me for, the depression that consumed me. What good was all this equipment if I didn't want to live?

Despite the support from loved ones, I struggled deeply with the loss of my identity. Being a mother felt like it had been taken away from me as I depended on others to care for my daughter. I was thankful for friends and family who stepped in to provide daycare and take her to sleepovers, but it broke my heart to be so disconnected from her daily life. I constantly worried about how this upheaval would impact her development and well-being.

The days that followed were filled with small victories and ongoing struggles. Each day presented new challenges in managing secretions and stridors, but it also offered moments of joy and progress as I continued to walk further distances.

Another Swallow Test

Another milestone I desperately wanted to achieve upon returning home was to regain the ability to eat and drink by mouth, freeing myself from tube feedings. The following week, I returned to Desert Regional for another Modified Barium Swallow Study, filled with hope that the countless hours of tedious and monotonous swallowing exercises had finally paid off.

Nervously, I sat in the familiar swallow chair as Dale stepped aside, following the usual protocol.

The speech therapist greeted me and the exam began. As I was served teaspoon after teaspoon of barium, that chalky white substance that the swallow study team watched on the monitors, I tried to remain hopeful and positive, but it was incredibly difficult.

We worked our way through more trials this time and that made me hopeful. However, the speech therapist explained that I still was aspirating my liquids and my throat wasn't cleanly swallowing my food trials. She recommended continued tube feedings. The diagnosis of being NPO (nothing by mouth) again crushed my spirits. All the relentless effort seemed in vain. I wondered if I would ever again drink a glass of cold water. I just couldn't imagine.

A Joyful Reunion

Wanting to see my school team and personally share my story with each of them, I decided to attend one of our monthly department meetings. The decision was nerve-wracking, but I felt it was necessary, and I so desperately wanted that connection. I asked Dale and my mom to go with me: Dale for support and my mom because she worked in the school for 20 years and knew many of my SLP friends.

The day of the meeting, a friend came over to help me dress and do my hair and makeup, creating a facade that masked my deepest depression and grief. I was looking and acting the best that I could, but it was all an act. I just needed this little win.

When I arrived at my school district office where meetings took place, I remembered that the meeting was upstairs. The elevator was still out of order, but I reassured myself that I could do this. With each slow, deliberate step up the stairs, my heart pounded, and my breath grew short. I gripped the hand railing tightly with one hand and held onto Dale with the other, leaning on him for support.

I made it step by step, and as I opened the door, everyone gasped in surprise. Overwhelmed, I fell against the door in tears. My mom caught me before I collapsed, and my lead SLP, Dana, rushed to my side, guiding me to my team. They embraced me with genuine love and support.

I sat down and Dana handed me the microphone. Holding it, I cried as everyone watched with tears in their eyes, waiting for me to speak.

I recounted my experiences to a room full of SLPs, sharing what I had been through as an SLP. It was a surreal moment and time stood still. I described the reality of the MBSS, the grief of dealing with a neurological disorder, and my deep appreciation for their support through texts and calls over the past few months.

By sharing these experiences, I hoped to bridge the gap between academic learning and real-life practice, offering my colleagues a deeper understanding of the human side of speech-language pathology.

At the end of the day, as I reflected on my outing, I felt a deep sadness.

I no longer seemed to fit into the professional world I once knew. I no longer seemed to fit in anywhere.

The memories of playdates, being in the working world, being actively involved in my child's life, and going out to lunch with work colleagues felt like they belonged to a past life. I struggled to relate to those aspects of my former self.

It was a harsh reality to face. My life had changed so drastically that the person I used to be felt lost, buried beneath the weight of everything I had endured.

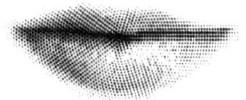

CHAPTER 10
The Emotional Battle of Recovery

The emotional battle of recovery was relentless. I had to continuously remind myself to be patient, accepting that progress would be slow, and setbacks were part of the journey.

The stridors were becoming more frequent, mostly occurring at night as I was drifting off to sleep. I became increasingly anxious and fearful of falling asleep, knowing that the episodes were more likely to happen during those vulnerable moments. I still relied heavily on my suction device, which I hated with a passion.

The support from my family was unwavering. My parents were a constant presence, helping with my daughter and providing their love and encouragement. It brought me continual peace knowing she was with them, receiving invaluable love and attention.

Even though I missed spending time with her, I had to remind myself that my parents were gaining precious moments with her, which was a gift in itself. However, the constant ripple effect of how my nightmarish situation was weighing on everyone around me was always on my heart and mind. I felt deep sadness and grief for dragging others into the hell I was living in. None of us had asked for this.

Support from the community also played a crucial role in my recovery as well. Dale's work clients stepped up, offering rides to infusion appointments, spending countless hours walking with me, and accompanying me to the gym, all without really knowing who I was. Their generosity and support were astonishing.

My colleagues from work also made a difference by scheduling themselves to take me to doctors' appointments, which occupied most of my days. If I wasn't at the doctor's, I would spend my time sleeping, reading cards from prayer warriors, and doing home therapy exercises with the bands and pulley cables I bought off Amazon.

During that time, Dale spent his days fighting with insurance to get home health services started and to get the necessary medical equipment and supplies for feeding that I desperately required. He was relentlessly fighting for me every step of the way and he shared in my fear of the unknown, but his determination never wavered. He remained hyper-focused on securing the best possible services, driven by a love and hope that I would have every chance at a full recovery.

As I settled into the routine of home health OT, PT, and speech services, I realized how much I had taken for granted before my illness. Simple tasks like getting dressed, brushing my teeth, and even walking required tremendous effort and assistance. The whole process was humiliating.

The physical limitations were frustrating, but the emotional toll was even greater. I often found myself lost in thought, grieving the loss of my former self and the life I once knew, wondering why I hadn't died in the ICU. I couldn't stop thinking, "What happened to me?" and "Why didn't I just die?"

Home health services proved to be eminently frustrating. Scheduling the appointments and waiting for the therapists to show up, just to do the exercises at home that I already knew how to do, felt fruitless and like a waste of my time.

A Slow Spiral into Depression

My mental health was deteriorating by the day. I knew I needed to find a therapist to help me process all the trauma I had been through. Finding such a therapist who understood medical trauma was challenging, and many fell short. Friends and family often didn't know what to say, leaving me feeling like the elephant in the room. I wished there were a guarantee that I would get my previous life back, but there was no guarantee that things would ever "return to normal," adding to my depression.

I did work with one therapist who helped me navigate some of the complex emotions I was experiencing. We did hypnosis and EMDR Therapy, with little change. I even tried cognitive behavioral therapy (CBT). The stress I was under and the losses were just too great to handle. While she was very good, I simply needed more than what she offered.

I wasn't sure I wanted to live like this any longer. No one understood me, and I was living in a world I didn't fit into. No one around me understood my new reality, and they all slipped further away from me. I knew I had to find a new community, a community of people who understood me, when my once-close friendships started to dissipate.

I also worried that come fall, everyone's life would return back to normal as the school year started, and my path in the rehabilitation world would continue, further leading me to feel alone and isolated.

Being home now, I knew it would be important to start resuming some typical activities out in the community. I was not able to drive but, with others' help, I was able to slowly make it into a store. I'd return home in frustration as I quickly came to realize that I no longer fit into this world and being out in public caused anxiety and exhaustion.

My daughter, still living with my parents, spent her days in preschool and afternoons at playdates, allowing me to attend in-home therapy sessions or simply rest. I desperately wanted to resume the normal activities of being a mom, but I felt like I had fully lost my identity, as I was still unable to do most things I wanted to do. The depression escalated as each day I had to come to grips with my new life. But I was deeply grateful that she was in good hands with my parents.

My days no longer revolved around work, playdates, shopping and preparing meals, or tucking my daughter in at night. Instead, they were consumed by therapy sessions, medical appointments, and overwhelming fatigue. The vibrant, active mom I once was felt like a distant memory, replaced by a version of myself that I hardly recognized. It was as if the essence of who I was had been stripped away, leaving me feeling empty and disconnected from the life I once knew.

I cherished the times when my daughter was home with me, but they also revealed a profound state of guilt and sadness. I could only engage with her from the couch, feeling a deep sense of loss as I watched her play and explore without me. I longed to get on the floor with her, to join in her games and outdoor activities, but my physical limitations kept me confined to watching.

The absence of those joyful moments together was a heavy burden on my heart. I missed the connection and fun we used to share. However, the quality time we spent napping each day provided a small comfort amidst the sorrow, reminding me that even in my current state, our bond remained strong.

Every morning, I would wake up and continue my walking routine, now covering four laps around my cul-de-sac. Even in the near 90-degree summer heat, I pushed myself to keep going. The sun beat down relentlessly and the air felt heavy and oppressive.

Despite the conditions, I found a sense of accomplishment in each step, knowing that every lap brought me closer to my recovery goals. The heat was challenging, but it also became a part of my daily routine, a testament to my determination and resilience.

During these walks, I would look at the hills in the distance and think about jumping off one of them to end my life, to avoid taking another step or participating in another therapy session. Each day was a struggle, full of pain and discomfort, and I would count down the hours until nap time, when I could escape my thoughts and snuggle up with my daughter.

I looked forward to those hours of sleep, shutting off my mind and escaping from my reality.

Once the temperatures became more extreme, I switched to walking at the local mall in the early morning with my mom or friends. The break in scenery provided the mental health lift I needed, and spending time with friends was also a good distraction. The change of environment and company helped me feel more connected and less isolated, giving me a sense of normalcy and support.

More and More Follow-up Appointments

UCSD scheduled various follow-up appointments for me within a month of my discharge from rehab to check on my progress. We anxiously got in the car for another trip down the road. Knowing this journey and seeing my former hospital environment would bring back vivid reminders of my recent past. I approached it with a mix of fear and hesitation, preparing myself for the emotional and physical challenges that laid ahead.

As Dale and I drove the nearly three-hour trip to San Diego, I felt every bump and turn in the road. Neither Dale nor I spoke, both lost in our thoughts as usual. Car rides had become excruciatingly painful, and I had to recline my seat and wear a soft neck brace to manage the discomfort.

We had to stop halfway so I could get up and move. The winding road over the hill, notorious for its frequent accidents, brought dark thoughts to my mind. Each sharp curve and sudden drop made me imagine our car losing control, plunging off the road, and ending my suffering in an instant.

These thoughts were disturbingly vivid. I pictured the release from pain and the finality of it all as a way to escape the relentless torment of my new reality. But despite these thoughts, I knew I wanted Dale to survive and to continue raising our daughter. The drive was filled with silence.

When we finally arrived, we stayed overnight at a home within walking distance of the beach. Knowing we would be down there for the week attending appointments, my parents brought my daughter so we could have a beach day and spend some time together as a family.

Despite the idyllic setting, I felt a grave sense of loss as I watched my daughter play on the playground. I wanted to be the active mom I once was, pushing her on the swings and climbing the monkey bars with her, but all I could do was sit and watch from a distance, taking pictures and pretending to be happy.

Faking joy started to become such a burden. My mind was consumed with my upcoming appointments and the grief of being such a burden to everyone around me.

I was consumed with fear about my first appointment of the day, afraid of what they were going to say and have me do. I worried that they would request another brain MRI which would indicate that I had a terminal brain disorder. As we walked back to the house to load into the car, a wave of heat swept over me and I started throwing up in the park. Embarrassed and unable to stop, I felt exposed.

When we made our way back to the car, and my mom and dad took our daughter back to the house where we were staying, while Dale and I headed to the first appointment of the day. As we got into the car, it was a quiet ride; both of us were filled with nerves and uncertainty about what lay ahead. When we arrived, Dale got out of the car, opened my door, and gently helped me out, never letting go of my hand as we walked inside the building. Though we were each lost in our own thoughts, we felt connected — together, unified in facing whatever was to come.

A Possible Diagnosis

Meeting the new neurologist was nerve-wracking. As we arrived at the office, the weight of the unknown and my deep anxiety overwhelmed me. The stress was so intense that I felt a wave of nausea wash over me, and before I knew it, I was vomiting again, this time in the parking lot. My stomach churned with dread at the thought of her requesting another brain MRI, and the fear that a bone protrusion I felt on the back of my head might be a brain tumor consumed me. Each moment felt like an eternity as I struggled to regain my composure and gather the strength to face what was ahead. The uncertainty of the situation weighed heavily on me, making it difficult to breathe as I braced myself for whatever news the neurologist might deliver.

In the waiting room, I sat silently, observing the other patients and wondering whether they noticed how out of place I felt. Eventually I was called back to the examination room. The neurologist, Dr. Corey-Bloom, introduced herself and began reviewing my notes while asking detailed questions. I explained my neck pain and weakness, my paralyzed arm, and my fear of the unknown.

I cried. She listened attentively, typing on her computer and occasionally looking up to ask more questions. She asked me to walk up and down the hallway, observing my gait.

When she finally mentioned Guillain-Barré Syndrome, specifically the pharyngeal-cervical-brachial variant (PCB-GBS), I was struck by a mix of shock and relief. After four long months of uncertainty and anxiety, hearing an official diagnosis was both a jolt and a beacon of hope. Finally, there was a name for my condition, providing clarity and a path forward.

The relief of having a diagnosis was profound, even as the reality of the condition sank in. Initially, I disregarded the diagnosis as I vividly recalled being tested for GBS in the ICU setting and that the possibility was ultimately excluded. She quickly dismissed my doubts, explaining the differences between the variant they tested me for and the variant I specifically had. After her description, I realized how accurate she was.

Dale was also relieved to finally have an accurate diagnosis. I could see him shifting into his usual "problem-solving" mode, focused on what he could do next to ensure the best outcome. He took meticulous notes and asked questions, determined to make sure Dr. Corey-Bloom was thorough and precise. Meanwhile, I sat there, speechless, feeling a mixture of relief and uncertainty.

She said the recommended treatment protocol for GBS was a procedure called Intravenous Immunoglobulin (IVIG). She further explained that I would need to start treatments immediately and that recovery would be a long, hard process. While it was comforting to have a diagnosis, my fears and pain were still very real. We left her office feeling a sense of accomplishment and progress, but my fear of the future remained.

After the appointment, we had to visit a pulmonary doctor's office, where I underwent various tests. My respiratory control was weak, and I felt defeated after failing most of the tasks. That night, a stridor episode woke me up right as I started to drift off to sleep, adding to my growing list of anxieties.

Experiencing the stridors was terrifying. Their harsh, grating characteristic sound was caused by an obstruction in the upper airway. An episode felt like my vocal cords were seizing up, making it hard to breathe and causing a panic that only made it worse. I didn't feel my difficulties were getting any better with time, and I worried about my future and the future of my family.

While I was there, I also reconnected with my husband's trainer who had visited me weeks earlier in the ICU. She offered innovative and challenging workouts designed to restimulate my nervous system and find new neural pathways. I loved my time with her as she was positive and encouraging.

She also addressed the nutritional aspect of my healing, helping me get on a protocol of supplements that Dale could grind up and put in my tube. I continued to see her throughout my journey, driving down every few weeks for new challenging workouts.

I came home that afternoon exhausted from the day's events. My family gathered around the dinner table and began eating, drinking, laughing, and talking. I wondered if they realized how easy it was for them to eat and drink.

Since I was still not eating or drinking anything orally, I sat to the side, reflecting on the day, feeling alone, isolated, and angry that I no longer fit in. After dinner, Dale tube-fed me outside in an attempt to hide the procedure from everyone else. I worried that my daughter would see my tube and ask questions, and I wasn't prepared to have that conversation with her yet.

That night, as I drifted off to sleep, a stridor episode hit me. I sprang up out of bed, unable to breathe. I tried the strategies taught by my SLP, but the vocal folds would not relax back into their normal rhythm. It was terrifying. Crying and trembling with fear, I sat at my bedside looking at my husband in terror, afraid to go back to sleep.

I did not know how to manage these stridor episodes and felt badly that he had to watch me go through them. After what felt like hours, my breathing settled down and my vocal folds began functioning normally again, and I was able to breathe. I was finally able to sleep. We both were.

The next day we woke up and prepared for another day of follow-up appointments. We had an appointment scheduled with the ICU Recovery Clinic. I wasn't sure what this was for, but I attended nervously, nonetheless. A young doctor entered the room and introduced herself as Dr. Bellinghausen, mentioning that she recognized me from the ICU and had recommended I come in for a brief evaluation and consultation.

She told me about the clinic's purpose and asked me how I was doing since she last saw me. I looked at her and cried, feeling completely shattered. How does one answer that question when every aspect of your future has been upended? When the life you once envisioned – filled with dreams, goals, and hopes – had been abruptly taken away? How can you put into words the profound sense of loss and despair?

"I often wish I had died," I told her, tears streaming down my face. She looked at me, and I could tell that her heart sank.

She administered a cognitive test called the Montreal Cognitive Assessment (MOCA), which brought a fleeting smile to my face as I recalled my grad school days spent completing clinical hours. I passed the test, as I had anticipated, but it became clear that my struggles went beyond cognitive issues; I was profoundly depressed.

Dr. Bellinghausen then explained a diagnosis I had never heard of before: post-intensive care syndrome (PICS). She told me that PICS encompasses a range of impairments that can affect patients after their ICU stay. She explained that physically, individuals may experience muscle weakness, decreased endurance, and difficulties with mobility due to prolonged bed rest and critical illness. Cognitively, they might face challenges with memory, attention, and decision-making, which can impact their daily functioning and responsibilities. And if that wasn't enough, psychologically, PICS can lead to anxiety, depression, and post-traumatic stress disorder (PTSD), stemming from the traumatic ICU experience and the stress of recovery.

When she mentioned PTSD, anxiety and depression, my curiosity peaked; her words started to make sense and resonate deeply with how I was feeling. This explained a lot and helped clarify the confusing and distressing symptoms I had been experiencing. At least now, I had a diagnosis and a path forward. She recommended joining a virtual support group and scheduled a follow-up appointment for later in the summer.

Diagnosing Vocal Fold Dysfunction

I returned home feeling utterly exhausted, overwhelmed, and anxious – emotions that had become all too familiar after a grueling week of medical appointments. My stress was elevated to a level that was off the charts, constantly gnawing at me and making every day a challenge.

The constant pressure and anxiety made it difficult to find any peace. The only respite I found from this relentless stress was in my daily naps. Those brief moments of sleep offered me a precious escape, allowing me to temporarily disconnect from the overwhelming chaos and recharge, even if just for a short while.

The next day we had a follow up appointment with an ear, nose, and throat (ENT) doctor. I arrived at the appointment and when the doctor walked in, he was smiling and said, "I'm not sure you remember me, but I saw you in the ICU. Every year I have a patient comes in as a medical mystery and you are that patient for me this year." We chatted for a bit, and I felt he really cared. I told him about my stridor episodes, and he said, "Let's take a look at your throat and see what's going on."

I don't remember the details of the scoping procedure, but I do remember him telling me I had something called PVFM, or paradoxical vocal fold movement disorder. He explained that PVFM is a voice disorder that occurs when the vocal cords close when they should be open for breathing. He further explained that this can cause difficulty breathing and talking, and can lead to a number of symptoms, including my stridor episodes and the reason why my voice now had a higher pitch overall. I welcomed this new information, as it added answers to some of my questions.

Later that week, I nervously attended my first virtual PICS support group. Unsure of what to expect, I felt apprehensive, as I had never been one to sit around a group forum and openly discuss my feelings. Nevertheless, I knew I needed something because my depression seemed to deepen with each passing day. The support group provided me with a sanctuary where I could voice my deepest concerns and fears about my recovery. Anna, a social worker was the moderator and introduced a weekly topic for us to discuss. We often found ourselves drifting off-topic, as many of us had so many heart-wrenching stories to share. We'd cry, laugh, and encourage each other, and I'd often leave the session feeling immense relief, surrounded by people who understand this new version of me.

Surrounded by fellow survivors of critical illnesses, I found a community that truly understood my struggles with depression and anxiety. They have been a big part of the community I so badly needed during my journey. The group not only offered emotional support but also equipped me with practical strategies for managing the stress I was under and navigating the emotional trauma, isolation, and grief I faced. Jess, another social worker, took over the group a couple of years later and continued to create safe spaces for us to share and heal. Despite the physical distance between us, many of these individuals have become some of my closest friends. Our shared experiences have fostered deep connections and a unique sense of camaraderie. In our virtual meetings, we not only offer each other support but also share personal stories and coping techniques, which has strengthened our bonds.

On my most challenging days, the encouragement and check-ins from group members via text or phone call have been invaluable. I often wonder where I would be today without their unwavering support, available at all hours. These friendships remind me that I am not alone on this journey; we all face our own battles, yet together, we find solace and strength. Each person's story is a testament to resilience, and their understanding presence is a constant reminder that we are all navigating this path together.

Back to the Urgent Care Where It All Began

Another referral that came in was to start intravenous immunoglobulin (IVIG), a treatment that involves administering a concentrated collection of antibodies to a patient through a drip. It's used to treat a variety of conditions, including immune disorders, autoimmune disorders, infections, and inflammatory conditions. My treatments were to start off at three consecutive days per month for a year and then taper off over the next three years.

The treatments were conducted at the urgent care facility I originally went to more than four months ago, where it all began, where I was given anti-nausea medication and IV fluids to address GBS, which they didn't know was GBS at the time. I couldn't help but wonder, if they had given me IVIG that day instead of anti-nausea meds, would my outcome have been different?

I went into that first appointment with extreme anxiety. Entering that building was like walking back in time, reliving the events of the previous months. I was hot, and my state was fueled by anxiety and depression. The nurse took me back, and as they collected my vitals, I cried.

She read my chart and history and offered to pray for me. Wow. I couldn't believe it. She looked at me tearfully and said, "I will continue to pray for you." I was so deeply grateful for her honest and heartfelt compassion. I didn't feel like a medical number to her. She genuinely cared.

I was then passed on to another medical professional, who asked me to complete additional paperwork regarding whether or not I wanted a Do Not Resuscitate order and related paperwork. This meant that if things didn't go well, I didn't want life-saving measures to be taken and I would be allowed to die. Sitting at his desk, he gave me the papers and asked me to sign them.

I sat there, staring blankly at him, unable to speak. I turned my head, staring out the window to my side for minutes on end. I had no energy or desire to engage with him or complete these papers.

Finally, after a minute of silence, I looked at him and Dale and said, with a slight tremor in my hands and quiver in my voice, "I can't do this right now." Dale sat there silently, not knowing what to say but letting me make the decisions as to what I wanted to do. Not answering, I got up and proceeded to the next room to begin my infusion. I sat down in the chair, emotionally depleted by the events surrounding me.

My nurse appeared and introduced herself as Vanessa. We exchanged a friendly conversation about having the same name and joked that I would receive such good care because she had such a great name.

I felt at ease as she got my medication ready. I informed her that ICU life had really damaged my veins and that I hoped she was successful on the first attempt, knowing it was highly unlikely. She got some heating packs and placed them around my arms as they would often do in the ICU setting.

The warmth from the heating packs increases blood flow to the area, making the veins more prominent and less likely to collapse when a needle is inserted. This technique is especially helpful in patients like me with damaged or fragile veins, as it improves the chances of successfully inserting an IV on the first attempt.

My anxiety grew as she prepared to insert the needle, knowing how fragile my veins had become. As could have been expected, the first prick to my arm caused my vein to collapse. I felt immediate worry and frustration, and when a sensation of warmth arose throughout my body, I knew I was about to faint. After a brief moment of unconsciousness, when I came to, the nurses were fanning me. They reclined my chair and tried again. She got it on the next attempt, and I knew it worked when I tasted the saline flush. Now it just needed to hold up for three days.

Unfortunately, the IVIG treatments didn't seem to make any noticeable difference, so I continued to do my assigned strengthening and range-of-motion workouts at home, which also felt like they were going nowhere. In hindsight, the treatments and workouts were all about reactivating those damaged neural pathways, and the lack of perceptible progress was an indication of just how long this recovery process would take.

I continued to receive a tremendous amount of support from my prayer warriors, and I was deeply grateful for their continued encouragement. I loved sitting on the couch and opening their cards each afternoon.

Despite this, I still felt isolated. I persisted with hypnosis, EMDR, and cognitive behavioral therapy, even adding antidepressants to the mix to help with the depression I was experiencing, but nothing seemed to provide the relief I was hoping for. The antidepressants triggered a new set of symptoms, including a racing heart rate that made me question whether I was experiencing a heart attack.

Amidst this struggle, attending my weekly PICS virtual support group seemed to be a beacon of hope. My new village of virtual supporters, alongside my prayer warriors, helped me navigate some incredibly dark moments.

The reassurance that I wasn't alone and the reminder that God was in charge and healing me offered a comfort that nothing else could. The stories shared in the group resonated deeply with me, providing a connection and solace that helped me endure. This was my new peer group, I told myself.

Small Signs of Recovery

I weaned off all medications and decided to focus on natural healing methods. Dale took on the responsibility of making my tube feeds from scratch, ensuring that we knew exactly what was going into my body. He dedicated so many hours to pureeing salmon, organic chicken, beef, sweet potatoes, and steamed vegetables into a liquid consistency for safe administration into my stomach.

I dreaded the moments when I had to wait for him to feed me. The process of lifting my shirt and exposing my tube to him for life-saving nutrition was both deeply humbling and yet embarrassing.

Each feeding brought with it depression and sadness, constantly reminding me of my dependency on him for even the most basic needs. It was a stark reminder of how much my identity and sense of self had been stripped away.

Seeing the worry and exhaustion in Dale's eyes was painful, knowing that my condition placed an immense burden on him. What should have been a comforting act of care only intensified my feelings of loss and helplessness.

My arm strength was improving very slowly, gaining just a millimeter of movement at a time. Doubts about whether it would ever fully recover lingered in my mind. Until one day, during nap time, I found myself unable to sleep.

As I laid there with my daughter by my side, a moment came that I will never forget. I mustered all my effort to lift my arm, feeling as if I were pushing against the weight of a bus. The exertion was immense; my arm trembled with every inch it rose. My muscles burned and ached, and I could feel every fiber straining under the effort.

Breathing heavily, I managed to get it up toward the ceiling. I held it there, but the weight became unbearable, and my arm gradually toppled back down. Despite the exhaustion, I was overcome by the sheer excitement of making progress and, for the first time, felt that my arm would indeed recover.

I immediately got out of bed and called Dale, eager to share my accomplishment with him, knowing that this small victory meant so much more. I sent my prayer warriors a video of it and they were overjoyed with the progress, thanking God for healing my frail body.

Small signs of recovery were starting to show, even though they were all so minuscule. I was relieved to have gotten to the point where I no longer needed the neck brace and commode. I despised those items with a burning hatred – the neck brace had felt like a constant reminder of my disability and the bedside commode had been a symbol of my lost independence.

The day I was able to throw them away was filled with immense satisfaction and joy. It felt liberating to discard them, a small but significant victory in my recovery. I looked forward to the day that the shower chair and suction machine were no longer a part of my life.

I was fearful of being left alone, terrified that a stridor episode would start and leave me unable to breathe. Because of this, Dale was unable to tend to any duties outside the house until I was supervised.

This added immense sadness to my life, knowing I had become such a burden in so many ways to others.

The guilt and sorrow weighed heavily on me, feeling as though my condition was pulling everyone down. Friends would come by, wash my hair, style it, or simply hang out and watch a movie with me so I wasn't alone. My mom would come by and clean our house, tidying up so Dale didn't need to. While I was deeply grateful for their help, the overwhelming sense of being a burden never left me.

Mealtimes were exceptionally difficult and I dreaded them. The food always smelled wonderful and made my mouth water ever more, knowing I wouldn't be able to eat it. I tried to conceal my sadness while watching everyone else gathered around the table, devouring a meal without the fear of choking. It made me feel terribly alone, and I sat on the couch as they ate, further exacerbating my depression and isolation.

It was one of those things you didn't truly understand until you experienced it yourself. I hoped outpatient speech therapy would jumpstart my progress or that I would wake up one day to find my muscles responding again. However, with each passing day, the hope and positivity kept fading.

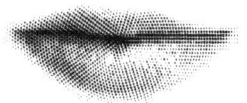

CHAPTER 11
Finding Strength in My Trials

When insurance finally approved outpatient therapy, I had high hopes that it would have a positive impact on my recovery. However, the logistics of getting to these appointments turned out to be complicated. I had to rely on friends for rides, which added another layer of difficulty to the process. Managing transportation was a constant challenge and the reliance on others for these essential trips added to my stress. Despite the hurdles, I remained hopeful that the therapy would bring meaningful progress.

To add to my stress, my outpatient therapy was scheduled back at Eisenhower Medical Center, the very place where my journey had begun and where I was first admitted. The thought of returning there stirred up a whirlwind of emotions, from anxiety to dread. It was unnerving going back to the place where it all started. Flashbacks to the night I drove there in the dark, seeing the familiar buildings of when I was declining and the uncertainty of what was happening to my body 2 months before made me cry at the sight. Flashbacks and PTSD were alive.

My therapy sessions also provided Dale with much-needed time to tackle the tasks he needed to take care of for himself. I knew it was a relief for him to have the support of others who were willing and able to pitch in and help when needed.

I worried about his mental and physical health. Being a caregiver is grueling, and I was deeply concerned about the toll it was taking on him. Seeing him juggle his responsibilities and care for me, I understood the immense pressure he was under and hoped he was dealing with it OK amidst the demanding circumstances. He was a stoic, problem-solving man, and he did not easily express his emotions.

My first outpatient speech therapy session was scheduled and I was excited to be working with an SLP named Sherry, a respected speech therapist I had heard so much about from colleagues. I was surprised, though, when another SLP started our session. She was nice and professional, but the anxiety of not having the therapist I had expected led to a stridor episode, heightening my stress.

I was embarrassed but unable to control it. She looked at me with big eyes and a panicked expression, unsure of how to approach the situation. I felt bad for her. We left without gaining any new knowledge or trying any new strategies for improving my voice or swallowing abilities. Our lack of progress was due to the stridors prominent during the session, not due to any lack of skill or expertise on her part. I was devastated.

At the start of my next speech therapy session, Sherry walked into the room, and I felt a wave of relief. She quickly assessed my condition and mentioned that she had reviewed my previous MBSS report.

With a reassuring smile, she said, "Let's get you eating. The best way to strengthen those muscles is to eat food!" This was a revelation for me – no one had ever approached my therapy with such fearlessness and urgency before. I was nervously optimistic and turned over all control to her to get me eating again.

We started with pudding and sips of water. Sherry's method was different from what I had experienced previously. This new direction was both exciting and daunting. Her confidence in my recovery instilled a fresh sense of hope within me.

Each session with her presented new food choices and progress! Eating remained slow and awkward, especially with my paralyzed right arm, but I was finally making discernible progress. Sherry started me off with foods that were crunchy, like cheese and crackers and toast, to get me used to chewing again. We quickly progressed from there. That night, she sent me home with instructions to try eating a poached egg for dinner alongside my normal tube feed.

Although it felt good to taste flavors again, the experience was equally terrifying. I couldn't shake the thought: *What if I choked?* Even worse, the fear of choking and possibly dying right in front of my family haunted me. Every bite was a mix of hope and fear, as I navigated the journey back to eating solid food. Our goal was simple: to wean me from the feeding tube and begin meeting all my nutritional needs orally. A goal that seemed so simple, yet so far away.

I continued to wonder what it was like for her to treat another SLP, so I made sure to express my appreciation to her. I let her know how much her care and support meant to me, acknowledging her compassion and empathy for me and my family.

Therapy days were full days and after the speech therapy session, I went to PT and then OT. The therapists were both kind and compassionate, but the PT sessions were painful, often resulting in tears. Despite the pain, I pushed through the exercises, hoping for some progress.

I enjoyed my time with my OT because she had a wonderful personality, always made me laugh, and offered positive words of encouragement. Each session, she measured the distance my arm was moving, providing proof that with each passing week, I gained another centimeter of movement. I was grateful for this and had to remind myself that, even though the progress was slow and barely noticeable, I was indeed moving forward. Knowing that I was making progress brought a sense of relief, reassuring me that this was not my forever.

My favorite words from her were, 'Vanessa, there is no doubt you will regain full movement of this arm again; it will just take time and a lot of work.' Hearing this was comforting, and I was fully prepared to put in the effort.

I worked hard though, and I often came home feeling worse after PT requiring heating pads, pain-relieving ointment, and more pain medication. In the end, all those items provided little to no relief, and complete relief only came when I was asleep. I often wondered whether they were causing additional and unnecessary pain or if the pain was part of my healing journey, as the muscles remained terribly spastic.

Improvements in OT and PT were so minor it was hard for me to see, but those outside my immediate circle saw changes in me each time they saw me. My neck was stiff and immobile, and my right arm was still terribly weak. Each slow movement only came while lying down and with tremendous effort. These physical limitations were a constant source of frustration and fear.

These three outpatient therapies became a regular part of my routine, with sessions twice a week. Each three-hour visit was marked by both hope and frustration. Some days, I felt a glimmer of improvement; other days, it seemed like I was taking two steps backward.

The depression persisted, but the act of going out in public and attending therapy sessions provided some relief from the dark thoughts. Seeing the faces of my therapists brought some temporary happiness to my day, for which I was deeply grateful, even though they were unaware of the depth of the impact they had on me.

Prayer Warriors and PICS

The possibility of my illness returning haunted me, making it difficult to fully embrace the progress I was making. My mind was constantly thinking every twitch, pain, bump, or peculiar sensation was the illness returning.

I continued to find solace in reading the cards from my prayer warriors, which reminded me that recovery was possible but required hard work, faith in God, and a strong support system. My community of prayer warriors and friends who understood medical trauma helped me stay grounded and focused on my recovery.

I immersed myself in their positive thoughts and encouraging words and it carried me through many challenging times. I read their cards and personal stories, crying alongside them.

They celebrated each victory with me, no matter how small, and were the first ones I shared my progress with, including the moment I could finally raise my arm from a standing position. I even recorded a video of this milestone and eagerly sent it to them.

I continued with my weekly PICS support group. The attendees' stories confirmed that I wasn't alone and continually reminded me of the importance of community support in the healing process. They taught me that life can be cruel and unfair, but there is hope and a silver lining if you dig deep.

The group helped me gain perspective, reminding me to be grateful for the gifts each day brings because you never know what tomorrow will bring.

The depression continually grew, and I tried desperately to hide it from family and friends, putting on a fake mask of happiness, appreciation, and gratitude for being alive, but inside I kept wishing I were dead. The physical pain and grieving process were, at times, too much to bear. It wasn't easy, I won't lie. The depression and desire to be dead still lingered from the pain and discomfort of muscle paralysis.

Emotional Toll

As I made progress in speech therapy, the emotional toll of my condition weighed heavily on me. Dale was overwhelmed with managing insurance claims and doctor's appointments, while my mom took on the role of caregiver, handling daily tasks and household chores. I found myself depending on friends for basic needs, such as washing my hair or driving me to appointments. This loss of independence was both humiliating and deeply painful.

Reflecting on my close relationship with my own mom, I felt profound anxiety about my daughter missing out on the support and guidance only a mother could provide if I wasn't around. My mom was my pillar of strength, always offering unwavering love, wisdom, and encouragement. She was there for every milestone, setback, and triumph, providing comfort and stability. Her nurturing care had always shaped who I was, and I had relied on her advice and support throughout my life.

The thought of not being able to provide my daughter with the same level of care and support weighed heavily on my heart. I wanted to be there for her school achievements, heartbreaks, and victories. The idea of her growing up without my presence and missing out on the mother-daughter relationship that had been so crucial in my own life was devastating to me and weighed on my heart daily. I knew I had to keep fighting and not give up. She needed me.

On weekends, I arranged playdates for her, feeling immense guilt that I couldn't be the active, involved mother I once was. Even though my husband's clients and many friends had stepped up to help, I couldn't shake the feeling that my life would never return to normal and that I was forever missing out on being the mother I wanted to be.

Final MBSS, FEES, and PEG Removal

I continued to expand my oral food selection with Sherry's help and guidance. Each week, she would introduce new textures to my diet and, with every addition, I felt a bit of progress.

Sherry set an ambitious goal for me. If I could successfully maintain my weight and eat and drink only oral foods for a full 30 days without getting pneumonia, she would recommend a final MBSS to determine whether to keep the feeding tube or remove it.

This goal felt both daunting and intimidating, but despite my fears and uncertainty, I was more than willing to give it a try.

I was nervous, but each morning I would stand on the scale to check whether I was eating enough. Knowing that my body required additional calories to heal, I made sure to cover each meal with an extra layer of olive oil, coconut oil, or butter. I also supplemented with high-calorie cartons of Kate Farms organic tube feed as snacks.

It was an emotional rollercoaster, and the process of eating was exhausting. I worked tirelessly at reaching the goal, envisioning the day I would be able to eat again at the table with my family without feeling like an outcast.

After a lot of hard work, I managed to sustain my weight and only eat orally for a month without pneumonia or other signs of swallowing difficulties. It was an incredibly challenging period filled with immense fear and constant vigilance.

I monitored my weight daily, which remained stable – I didn't gain any weight but didn't lose any either. Worries plagued my thoughts: "What if I can't maintain my weight?" or "What if I lose weight and need the feeding tube reinserted?" Anxiety about these possibilities relentlessly entered my thoughts.

She now had me eating foods like enchiladas, yogurt, cottage cheese, and cream of wheat. I always added a layer of butter or olive oil for extra calories. I found that foods with a stickier texture went down best and relatively easily, which made me feel safer because they were less likely to get caught in my throat. Sherry even provided me with a recipe for a high-calorie pudding made from cashews and avocado, which was both nutritious and comforting.

There was a deep sense of satisfaction in eating these more familiar foods that I once enjoyed. It gave me a glimmer of hope for the future and filled me with excitement at the thought of being able to eat a meal at the dinner table with my family again.

I wanted so badly to be normal and join my daughter at the table, to share a meal with her like we used to. But with her boundless energy and enthusiasm, I just couldn't manage it. Eating required immense concentration, and her liveliness made it difficult to focus on the careful chewing and swallowing I needed to feel safe. To help me concentrate, I often tried to eat alone even when others were in the room.

Still, I couldn't help but worry how this entire experience might shape who my daughter would become in life. Would she remember me as distant, unable to fully join in her world? Would my struggles leave her feeling worried or fearful? These thoughts weighed heavily on me as I fought to regain my strength

One Final Swallow Study

After the month, as agreed, Sherry scheduled one final MBSS to ensure that the food and liquid was moving down through my throat as it should be and not diverting into my lungs. She needed to have "eyes on" my swallow before recommending the removal of my feeding tube.

On the morning of the test, I woke up with nervous anticipation. I felt confident, yet a small seed of worry lingered. I had become so accustomed to failed assessments that the prospect of success seemed almost surreal.

We drove to the hospital and were immediately taken back to the Radiology Department. Sherry was there offering a ray of sunshine as she explained what was going to happen. I sat fully erect in the swallow chair, praying this would be the last time.

She administered trial after trial of various barium consistencies. She ended the protocol by giving me a pill to swallow. I took it from her nervously, as this was one thing I never tried before. I put it in my mouth and took a large sip of water, hoping it would wash it down, but I immediately felt the sensation of it being lodged in my throat. I panicked.

Everything was going well until this. Calmly she instructed me to perform multiple hard swallows with sips of water. Eventually, it went down, and I felt a huge sense of relief.

"Everything looks good," she said happily. I am going to recommend you get your tube removed. I looked at her and smiled, something I rarely did anymore. Excitement was then replaced with nervous anticipation as I knew my lifeline for nutrition was going to be removed. I worried about the chance, even a small one, that I would need it reinserted.

Sherry's words struck a chord, resonating deeply with Dale. He felt his heart swell with a mix of pride, gratitude, and relief. His eyes brightened, his face lighting up with a combination of pride and humility. Hearing those words made him feel seen and appreciated in a way that cut through the exhaustion and worry he had carried for so long. It was as if Sherry's praise validated every late-night vigil, every moment of doubt, and every act of love he had poured into my care, making it all worthwhile.

Dale looked at her with a genuine smile, his eyes glistening with relief. "Thank you so much for everything," he said, his voice soft but overflowing with gratitude. As the words left his lips, his shoulders visibly dropped, as if a huge weight had finally been lifted from his heart. His whole body seemed to exhale, releasing the months of tension and anxiety that had held him captive. For the first time in what felt like forever, his mind was quiet, no longer racing with worry. He felt at ease and truly relaxed, the good news from Sherry washing over him like a calming wave, bringing a sense of peace he hadn't known in months

A Second Swallow Study to Confirm

As I was making progress in my eating, we had a follow-up appointment scheduled at the Voice and Swallow Clinic at UCSD. While there, we decided to seek a second opinion on whether I would be ready within the next week to have my PEG tube removed. The SLP, Kristin, agreed to conduct the assessment. I was nervous, as the last time I had a FEES (Flexible Endoscopic Evaluation of Swallowing) done was during a training seminar in grad school, where I fainted in front of everyone, causing extreme embarrassment.

Dale sat by my side as Kristin carefully inserted the scope into my nose and down my throat. She asked me to perform some swallows of a green, jelly-like substance. We both watched intently as the substance moved down my throat on the monitor in front of us. I silently prayed that everything would look good to her. When Kristin finally looked at us and said, "Yup, you look like you are ready to have your tube removed," a wave of relief washed over me. Hearing those words was a significant moment; it was the positive news I had been hoping for, marking a major step forward in my recovery.

Feeding Tube Removal

That day, Dale called the doctor to schedule the removal of my PEG tube. It was set to be removed the week before my birthday. While it should have been a reason to celebrate, I was terrified to the core of my being. I was deeply afraid that I wouldn't be able to maintain my weight and that the tube would have to be reinserted. The thought of potentially failing was daunting, overshadowing what was supposed to be a milestone in my recovery.

We drove to the doctor's office in silence, feeling uneasy about the procedure ahead, as it was uncharted territory for me. Upon checking in at the front desk, we were immediately taken back. I felt the usual wave of anxiety, causing me to perspire as I grappled with my fears.

When the doctor entered the room, he calmly explained the process of removing the tube. He put gloves on and gently lifted my shirt, revealing the white circular port protruding from my stomach. I couldn't wait to look down and see it gone, but the thought also terrified me.

In an instant, the tube was removed, and clear goo oozed from the hole now in my stomach. The doctor quickly wiped it away and placed a bandage over it. "That's it," he said. I was struck by how painless and quick the procedure had been.

Once it was over, I felt so much relief, although fear continued to linger for the rest of the day. I had to keep reminding myself that I could handle this and that this was just another moment to prove how mentally strong I was, that I was truly making progress.

I went home excited at the thought of eating again, but it also brought a new kind of stress. Dale took over the kitchen, making every meal himself. He poured olive oil, coconut oil, or butter over everything, determined to make each dish as calorie-dense as possible. I appreciated his dedication, but I could see the tension in his face — a mix of love and fear, hoping that every bite would help me heal just a little bit more. So much was riding on my ability to resume eating orally again.

Welcoming Routines Again

As fall arrived and everyone returned to their usual routines, isolation set in for me. Dale had to go back to work after seven months off and friends resumed their responsibilities. This transition was incredibly challenging, leaving me alone at home for long stretches.

Unable to drive, I felt confined and overwhelmed by solitude. The quiet hours forced me to reflect on my life and the stark reality of my condition. This intensified my emotional struggle, as I struggled with loneliness and a sense of being left behind.

I spent my mornings at the gym and my mom would come along to take me shopping in town. While walking around stores provided a welcome change of scenery and a chance to be around people, it was very taxing. I constantly worried about bumping into things due to my limited ability to fully rotate my head and body.

It was also physically and mentally exhausting. I noticed that being engaged in the community helped combat the depression, but when my daughter came by for afternoon visits – despite how much I longed to be with her – her boundless energy further exhausted me, exacerbating my depression once again.

I found myself anxiously looking forward to nap time, craving the rest and relief it brought from the constant exhaustion and pain.

I continued with my monthly IVIG sessions, not feeling even a slight change after each one. I wondered why I should continue with it at this point – the cost was outrageous, and the frustrations of going to the hospital every month only added to my depression. Despite my doubts, the neurologist was adamant that I shouldn't quit anytime soon.

Nine months later, I finally built up the confidence to drive again. I told my mom I wanted to try, and just like my first driving lesson, my dad came over and offered to drive with me. My neck had been gaining better range of motion every month since I'd left the ICU and, using mirrors, I was finally deemed safe to drive. My dad sat beside me, nervously chatting about this and that, his voice filled with a sweet attempt to take my mind off where I am on my journey. He was trying to reduce the worry and anxiety I felt about attempting to drive again, hoping to ease the tension that filled the car.

My first trip around the block was unnerving but exciting at the same time. It felt good to envision a future where I had a little more independence. The thought of being able to drive my daughter to school and get myself to the gym without having to rely on someone else was exhilarating. This small step forward filled me with hope and a renewed sense of freedom.

I drove back home, gently easing into the garage, where my mom eagerly greeted me. She wrapped me in a congratulatory hug, and we all felt a wave of relief wash over us, grateful for the success of my drive around the block. My parents were so happy for me as this was a huge milestone and they were so proud to cheer me on as I reclaimed my ability to drive.

My Return to Work with an Invisible Disability

The decision to return to work was filled with mixed thoughts. Dale and I discussed the pros and cons of returning and both felt it was a perfect time to ease back into the working world. Initially, I was reluctant, but when Covid-19 caused the world to come to a crashing halt, I quickly saw it as an opportunity to re-enter the workforce in a safe and manageable way.

Working from home made it possible; otherwise, I likely wouldn't have returned. The workload was relatively easy and expectations were significantly lowered as no one was sure how to proceed in this new uncharted territory the world was going through.

However, as restrictions regarding COVID were lifted, the pace picked up and things started to return to normal. We resumed a regular schedule, moving away from the virtual therapy I had been providing and back into a brick-and-mortar setting, providing therapy evaluations and services in person. At this point, everything changed dramatically for me as I had to deal with the challenges of an invisible disability.

Returning to my school, the elevator that wasn't working at the beginning of my medical journey was still out of order, forcing me to climb the stairs with all my materials despite my respiratory lung weakness, neck issues, and limb weakness. It wasn't the most ideal situation, but I persevered, not wanting anyone to know the major struggles I was dealing with.

My colleagues and the administration thought I was fine, but I was not. No one knew what I was secretly dealing with, and I made it a point not to discuss it. I looked fine but no one could see my internal scars. I did my job and went home, exhausted and in pain.

The first day back I made it a point to stay in my room and refamiliarize myself with my setting. I was afraid to see others and be judged, plus I was too exhausted to engage in conversation. The mental fatigue of being on campus and all the stimuli was exhausting. Coming back into my office for the first time was surreal. I walked in and looked around and cried. Everything was in total disarray. Additional furniture had been placed in my room, and I was not strong enough to move it.

I sat down in the chair, looked out my room window and cried. I wasn't even sure where to begin or how to make sense of all that had changed in my life. I didn't move for 30 minutes or so as I just sat there in disbelief over my life, reflecting on where I was the last time I was in that very same room. Everything was the same as how I left it, but I was not. I wasn't the same person. I sat down and cried for what was lost and for this new beginning.

In sadness and desperation, I texted my SLP friend, Ashley, who was working at the school site around the corner. She sensed my frustration and anger and came over, prepared to move furniture and do anything else needed to make my room functional again. I was so grateful for her understanding and responsiveness.

Final Notes

As the weeks turned into months and months turned into my one-year anniversary, I began to see more significant improvements. I knew my body would continue to heal if given the right tools, so I embarked on a mission to explore alternative therapies.

I was determined to regain what I had lost and trusted myself the most, so I decided to educate myself. I immersed myself in podcasts and books, read research articles, and reached out to experts in the field of biohacking. I talked to trusted professionals with values that aligned with mine. The concept of neuroplasticity and the modalities used by top experts to heal nervous system disorders fascinated me.

I decided to veer away from the mainstream medical route, which was a daunting decision. However, I continued with my IVIG treatments a year out, as my neurologist still wasn't comfortable discontinuing them. This balanced approach allowed me to blend conventional medicine with innovative therapies, fueling my hope and determination to recover fully.

Once I felt I understood enough, I began to develop a natural healing regimen. I tried weekly vitamin IV therapy, acupuncture, dry needling, and craniosacral therapy. I also tried endermologie, a massage technique that involves the use of a specialized device equipped with rollers and suction which gently massages and manipulates the skin and underlying tissues. Although these treatments were costly, they proved beneficial. My body needed an intense reboot. My body continued to progress, but as I knew, as it is with neurological deficits, the progress continued to be slow.

Additionally, I experimented with a few alternating current electrical stimulation devices, hoping they would aid in my recovery. I diligently used them, applying the electrodes to my body and following the recommended protocols.

Over time, I began to notice mixed results. Some days, I felt slight relief from the pain, but on other days, I experienced discomfort and increased pain and stiffness. The inconsistency made it difficult to determine the true efficacy of various therapeutic methods. After several months of trial and error, I decided to discontinue the use of alternating current therapies. It was a process of learning and adjusting, continuously seeking what worked best for my body.

Shortly after arriving home from the rehab facility, I connected with my trainer and we resumed working together. He added new workout programs to build strength and improve my range of motion.

One day, he introduced a new device to me that he had recently purchased, believing it could be a game changer for my rehabilitation. Though skeptical, I was intrigued and said, "Let's give it a try and see what happens!" I was always open to experimenting with different approaches for a few months, and if there were no noticeable gains, I would abandon them.

It was called the NEUBIE, a direct current (DC) electrical stimulation device. Unlike the alternating current (AC) devices I had previously used, the NEUBIE offered a wide variety of benefits for treating nervous system disorders.

As I normally do, I went down a rabbit hole, researching the differences in DC versus AC devices and how they would aid in helping my diagnosis of GBS. As he placed sticky electrodes on my right arm, cervical spine, and neck, my curiosity was piqued.

After the first session, I felt a distinct change. My body felt more relaxed, and my muscles were less stiff. Intrigued by this sensation, I decided to increase my appointments from once a week to twice a week, hoping to continuously activate and rewire my nervous system.

Within a month, I noticed significant improvements: I could lift heavier weights, rotate my body into new positions, and I felt a renewed sense of calmness.

The NEUBIE also helped my body move out of a state of fear and anger that had been hindering my healing, allowing me to shift from a constant state of stress and emotional turbulence to a more balanced, calm, and focused state.

This shift was crucial in enabling my body to engage in the healing process more effectively, as it alleviated the stress that had been impeding my progress.

The results were nothing short of amazing. I felt ecstatic and full of hope, as the NEUBIE breathed new life into my nervous system and contributed greatly to my journey toward recovery. I felt relief knowing that this journey and the pain and discomfort I was in wouldn't be mine forever.

As an SLP, I became fascinated by the potential of the NEUBIE as a crucial tool in healing nervous system disorders such as autism, multiple sclerosis, concussions, and strokes – all conditions which speech therapists treat.

Inspired by the progress, I decided to invest in my own NEUBIE. This decision marked a turning point, as having the device at home allowed me to continue my rehabilitation with greater consistency and control.

My journey had come full circle. From being a patient struggling to regain basic functions to becoming an empowered SLP, equipped with advanced tools and renewed purpose, I was ready to make a difference.

The NEUBIE was more than just a device; it was a symbol of resilience, hope, and the unyielding human spirit. With this newfound perspective and the support of my community, I looked forward to a future where I could help others reclaim their lives, just as I had reclaimed mine.

A New Beginning

At the time of this writing, I continue to live with the PTSD that affects so many ICU survivors. Various sounds and sights trigger vivid flashbacks to life in the ICU, causing me to quiver with anxiety and become tearful for where I was and where I am now. The PTSD leaves me with overwhelming feelings of fear and helplessness, bringing back the traumatic memories as if they were happening all over again.

These memories, no matter how much I wish I could erase them, will forever be a part of my past. I've had to learn and develop skills to manage these moments when they surface unexpectedly. Techniques like focusing on my gains, deep breathing, and practicing gratitude and mindfulness help me regain control, but the anxiety can still be overwhelming.

The ongoing struggle is not just about facing the possibility of physical relapse with Guillain-Barré Syndrome, but also about navigating the emotional toll of reliving those terrifying experiences. The fear and worry are continually there, and I will carry that burden for the rest of my life. It's a daily effort to remind myself to stay in the present, not to worry about the what-ifs, and to be grateful for today.

As I reflected on the journey detailed throughout this book, I was filled with a profound sense of gratitude and awe. The challenges I faced, the battles I fought, and the triumphs I achieved all contributed to a transformation I never imagined possible. This book has been more than a recounting of events; it has been a testament to the strength of the human spirit and the power of community.

This experience has profoundly changed my relationships with my family and friends. I am, without a doubt, a different person than I was before my medical journey. I've learned to appreciate the incredible resilience of the human body and the nervous system's remarkable capacity to heal. Simple moments that once might have passed by unnoticed now fill me with awe and gratitude.

When I watch my daughter do a cartwheel or a backbend, I am amazed at how strong and resilient her body is. Her movements are a reminder of the beauty of health and vitality, something I no longer take for granted. These small acts of strength remind me of my own journey, of the body's ability to recover and find its way back, even from the edge. I cherish our time together now more than ever, knowing that each moment is a precious gift. I find myself slowing down, truly listening to her, and appreciating the simple joys we share, recognizing how important it is to be fully present for her.

As a parent, these changes have had a profound impact on how I raise my daughter. I'm more intentional about the time we spend together, making an effort to be truly present with her. Whether we're reading a book, playing outside, or simply talking about her day, I focus on being fully engaged, not distracted by the hustle of everyday life. I try to teach her by example that what matters most is the love we share and the memories we create, not the things we own or the places we go.

I've become more patient, more understanding, and more compassionate, not just with her but with myself as well. I encourage her to explore, to take risks, and to embrace life with the same courage and resilience that I've had to find within myself. And in those quiet moments when she says, "I love you, Mommy," I hold her a little tighter, knowing that these are the moments that define a life well-lived.

This experience has also deepened my connection with my parents. They stood by me during my hardest times, their unwavering love and support serving as a lifeline when I needed it most. Now, our bond feels stronger, more genuine. I am more open and vulnerable with them, sharing my fears and hopes, knowing they understand in a way only parents can. I appreciate the sacrifices they've made and the depth of their love.

Our conversations are richer, filled with gratitude and mutual respect. We've come to cherish our time together, recognizing that the strength of our family lies in the love and support we give one another. In many ways, my journey has brought us closer, reminding me of the powerful role they continue to play in my life and how, no matter what, we face life's challenges together.

These are the moments that matter, the ones that remind us that life, with all its unpredictability and challenges, is still a precious gift. So, I try to embrace each day with an open heart, to let go of what I can't control, and to focus on the things and people that truly matter.

I have also learned that life isn't about material possessions but about quality time and community. Life is short, and the cliché that you never know what tomorrow will bring is undoubtedly true. I try daily to live as though today may be my last. This perspective has enriched my life in ways I never imagined. It has taught me to slow down, savoring the small joys and fleeting moments that truly matter. I've become more mindful, more present, and more appreciative of each day I have.

Additionally, I have developed a deep respect and admiration for individuals experiencing medical trauma and disabilities. Having walked a path of my own, I now understand more profoundly the challenges they face. Their strength, resilience, and perseverance in the face of adversity inspire me daily. I approach these experiences with empathy and an enhanced perspective, knowing that each person's journey is a testament to their courage and tenacity. This newfound understanding drives me to support and advocate for others in similar situations, hoping to offer the same compassion and encouragement that I have received.

The journey was far from easy, and there were moments when I doubted my ability to continue. However, with the unwavering support of my family, friends, medical professionals, and the countless prayer warriors who stood by me, I found the strength to persevere. Their love, encouragement, and belief in my recovery were the pillars of my strength, and for that, I am eternally grateful.

I've learned to appreciate the little things, those seemingly small moments that are often overlooked but hold so much meaning. My perspective has shifted dramatically, and the big things that used to consume me no longer hold the same weight. I've gained a clearer sense of what truly matters, distinguishing between what is genuinely a big problem and what is just a minor inconvenience. I've come to understand what's worth fighting for and what's better to let go. This shift in perspective has brought a sense of peace, as I now realize that not everything requires my energy and attention.

Through my experiences, I've discovered a strength within myself that I never knew existed. I've learned to fight with a tenacity I could have never imagined, to push through challenges with a fighting spirit that has become a core part of who I am. This journey has taught me what resilience looks like, and it's shown me the importance of facing life's battles head-on, even when they seem insurmountable, and you feel alone.

None of us can predict what the future holds, and that's why it's so important to find joy in today, even when the day is challenging. Life is fleeting, and we only get one chance to live it. Despite the cards we've been dealt, it's essential to figure out what brings us peace, what helps us navigate the tough times, and what allows us to keep moving forward.

Friendships have also taken on new meaning for me. I've come to value and cherish the time spent with people who genuinely add meaning and positivity to my life. I seek out connections that are nurturing, supportive, and filled with mutual understanding. These are the friendships that uplift me, offering comfort and strength during difficult times. By focusing on the people who truly matter, I've created a circle of friends who are not just companions, but true sources of inspiration and joy.

It's not always easy, but I've learned that even on the hardest days, there are moments of joy and gratitude to be found. Sometimes it's in a shared laugh, quality time with family, the comfort of a quiet morning, the gentle touch of a loved one's hand, the sounds of nature, the smell of fresh coffee brewing, or simply taking a deep, calming breath. These small but significant moments have also changed my relationship with my daughter, making me more patient, centered, and present.

Deeping Relationships with Dale, My Husband

Through all of this, my respect and love for Dale took on a new dimension. He was there for me in ways I never anticipated, stepping up without hesitation to face challenges neither of us were prepared for. His support wasn't flashy or over the top; it was in the small, steady actions he took every day — the phone calls to insurance, the endless questions to doctors, the calm reassurance when my own hope was wearing thin. Even when we were both exhausted and scared, he showed up, standing beside me, quietly doing whatever needed to be done. He didn't have to say much; his actions spoke louder than words. In those moments, I realized how much I relied on him, not just for the practical things, but for his steady presence, his commitment to being by my side through whatever came next.

This journey has reminded me of the critical role that communication plays in a marriage, especially when facing significant trauma. The experience has profoundly impacted my marriage to Dale. We were both thrust into a situation we never could have prepared for, with our lives turned upside down in a matter of days. Trauma like this can test even the strongest of relationships, as it brings out deep fears, vulnerabilities, and emotional pain that can be hard to navigate.

In moments of crisis, it's easy to become isolated, feeling like no one else can truly understand what you're going through. But I've learned that it's precisely during these times that open and honest communication becomes essential. It's not just about talking for the sake of talking but about really listening to each other, validating each other's feelings, and providing the support that only we can give each other as partners who are walking this path together.

Encouraging each other is also key. There have been days when one of us felt stronger and more hopeful, while the other struggled with fear and anxiety. In those moments, it's important to lift each other up, to remind ourselves of the progress we've made and the strength we've shown. A simple word of encouragement can make a huge difference and help the other person find the resilience to keep moving forward.

Being vulnerable, though incredibly scary, is crucial. Vulnerability involves exposing your deepest fears, your raw emotions, and the uncertainty you face in your new reality. It can feel like standing on a precipice, afraid that the slightest misstep might lead to a deeper emotional fall. Yet, it is this very vulnerability that allows us to truly connect and understand each other's pain and fears. It opens the door to authentic conversations about your struggles and hopes, which is vital for coping with the realities of your new life.

When we allow ourselves to be vulnerable, we invite the other person to share their own fears and anxieties without judgment. This mutual exchange creates a space where both partners can acknowledge their feelings and work through them together. It helps in coping with the emotional weight of trauma, as sharing these burdens can make them more manageable. Being vulnerable also fosters a deeper level of trust and intimacy, reinforcing the bond between the couple and affirming that you are not alone in this journey.

It can be incredibly beneficial to talk through the trauma, whether with each other, a therapist, or a Post-Intensive Care Syndrome (PICS) support group. Sharing experiences, expressing fears, and discussing the impact of trauma can help in processing what has been endured. These conversations not only provide a way to recognize that one is not alone but also show that others have faced similar challenges. Engaging in these discussions can be profoundly healing and can strengthen relationships, reinforcing the sense that you are navigating this journey together.

It's also important to remember that everyone handles trauma differently. Some may go into problem-solving mode, focusing on finding solutions and taking action, such as the way Dale did, while others like myself might experience depression, PTSD or anxiety. During these times, open communication is crucial to ensure that everyone is on the same page and understands each other's coping mechanisms. Being open about how each person is processing the trauma can help align efforts, provide mutual support, and maintain a unified approach to navigating the challenges ahead.

Overall, this experience has shown that communication goes beyond mere words; it's about deepening connection, building trust, and facing an uncertain future together. Even when words are hard, being present and showing empathy can make a huge difference. This journey has reinforced that, while trauma can challenge a relationship, open communication, mutual support, and vulnerability can help rebuild and even strengthen that bond.

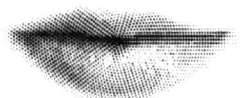

TO MY READERS

To my readers, I offer this message of hope: No matter the challenges you face, remember that you are not alone. Seek out your community of supporters, cherish the moments of kindness, and never underestimate your own strength. Life's obstacles may seem insurmountable, but with perseverance and support, you can overcome even the greatest of challenges.

As I look to the future, I am filled with optimism and determination. This book is not just about my journey; it is about the incredible community that came together to support me. It is a reminder that it takes a village to overcome adversity, and that together, we can achieve the extraordinary. Thank you for joining me on this journey. May you find strength in your own challenges, and may you always remember the power of community, resilience, and hope.

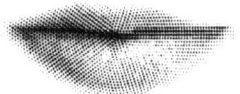

AUTHOR'S NOTE/DISCLAIMER

Due to the nature of my illness, the anxiety I endured, and the resulting PTSD from the trauma I experienced, my recollection of events and conversations during my two-month stay in the hospital is fragmented. Anxiety and PTSD can severely impact memory, often causing the mind to block out or distort certain events as a protective mechanism. As a result, many moments remain hazy or entirely blank, influenced not only by the effects of medication and intense pain but also by the overwhelming fear and anxiety that clouded my consciousness.

To piece together this story, I've relied on the evidence available to me: thousands of pages of medical records, recordings of modified barium swallow evaluations, numerous interviews with my medical team, and my personal journal entries written during recovery. I also reviewed hours of recorded therapy sessions to help reconstruct what was lost. While some identifying details have been altered, this memoir is a raw and honest account of my medical experience based on the memories I have.

However, despite extensive research and careful reconstruction, I recognize that my inability to be fully present during certain moments may have led to inaccuracies or omissions. I am, after all, a human being who has endured significant pain and trauma, and with that comes the potential for error. As humans, we are inherently fallible—our memories can be imperfect, our perceptions can be clouded by emotion, and our understanding of events can be shaped by the limitations of our experiences. While I have made every effort to present this account as truthfully and accurately as possible, I acknowledge that there may be things I didn't get right and many moments left unrecorded. This memoir is a testament to my journey, but like all human endeavors, it is not without its flaws.

Also, for the purpose of this book and for continuity, I have chosen to call the swallow test I experienced a Modified Barium Swallow Study (MBSS). It is also known as a Video Fluoroscopy Swallow Study (VFSS), and it should be noted that the University of California San Diego (UCSD) uses the term videofluoroscopy swallow study.

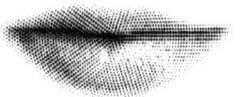

ACKNOWLEDGMENTS

This chapter of my life, marked by immense medical, emotional, and spiritual challenges, has also revealed the strength of my spirit and the profound importance of community. As I reflect on my journey, I am filled with immense gratitude for the family who stood by me, the medical professionals who cared for me, and the community that supported me. Their love and encouragement were the pillars of my strength, helping me to overcome even the greatest obstacles.

I dedicate this book to my husband, who has always supported me without hesitation, celebrating my successes and encouraging every endeavor I've pursued on my journey to healing. Your unwavering support has been my anchor, and your dedication to my well-being has been nothing short of extraordinary. Thank you for continually showing up and being my voice by advocating for me when I was unable to communicate. Your endless patience, strength, and resilience during the toughest times kept us both moving forward. You took action with remarkable determination, stepping up to the plate and tackling every challenge that arose. Whether it was negotiating with doctors, navigating insurance issues, or fighting for my health, you did so with unwavering resolve and tireless effort. May this book serve as a small token of my appreciation for everything you've done and continue to do, reflecting the depth of my gratitude for your relentless dedication and love.

To my incredible parents, whose love knows no bounds and whose wisdom guides me through life's twists and turns. Your unwavering support and steadfast belief in me have been my rock through every challenge and triumph. Thank you for not only standing by me but also for providing such loving and attentive care to my daughter. Your reassurance that she was safe and well cared for allowed me to focus on my healing without the constant worry about her well-being. You were always there for us, never saying no, no matter the time of day or the demands of the situation. Your readiness to help at a moment's notice, your boundless availability, and your unwavering dedication were truly extraordinary. This book is dedicated to you both, with heartfelt gratitude for the countless sacrifices you've made, the invaluable lessons you've taught me, and the boundless love you've shown to me and my family. Your influence has been a beacon of strength and inspiration, and I am forever grateful for all that you have given.

To Mel, my mother-in-law: Even though you were across the United States, you found a way to support me in the most unimaginable way by connecting me with my incredible prayer warriors. You graciously rose to the challenge and provided me with the gift of prayer that I often feel kept me alive. Your unwavering kindness and compassion for those in need make you truly one of a kind. I will always be grateful for your genuine, unconditional love and support.

To all my prayer warriors across the US for flooding me with cards and prayers. You gave me hope and reminded me that I wasn't alone in this journey and that God was behind the wheel. Your consistent support has been the foundation of my success and motivation to persevere through anything life throws my way. Thank you for never leaving my side and offering continual support and encouragement over the years. Each of you played a crucial role in my recovery, and I am forever grateful for your support.

To those who helped me write and edit this book, you were my cheerleaders, encouraging me to tell my story when I doubted myself the most. You pushed me at the right time, encouraged me, and wouldn't let me stop even when I doubted myself and my story. You were always willing and able to step up, offering your free time and words of encouragement. Thank you for believing in me. Your support and faith kept me going and made this book possible. From the bottom of my heart, I am grateful for each one of you.

To Mattie Murrey, my incredibly talented and supportive ghostwriter. You have a gift with words! I can honestly say I would have never had the confidence to step out and write this book if it hadn't been for your guidance and support. You have an extraordinary ability to capture and articulate exactly what I was thinking and feeling. Whenever I felt overwhelmed or felt like giving up, you would walk me off the ledge and remind me of how powerful my story was and never to give up. I appreciate you beyond words. Your texts of motivation and words of encouragement along this journey were what allowed this book to get done, and I am forever grateful for your supportive ways and friendship. (Find her at www.myownghostwriter.com)

To Dr. Jared Rosen, I am truly "speechless" when it comes to expressing my gratitude for your incredible support to Dale and me. The relief I felt seeing you stand by Dale's side, explaining complex medical procedures, and helping him navigate this journey without fear or intimidation was immense. Your support extended beyond just Dale and me; you also provided invaluable guidance and reassurance to my parents, offering them the comfort and clarity they needed during such a challenging time. You had the remarkable ability to see beyond the needs of my spouse and parents, recognizing that I was not just a patient but also a speech pathologist and mother who desperately longed to be with her child. You provided me with the tools to manage my anxiety about being apart from her, demonstrating a depth of understanding and compassion that meant everything to me. Your gift for communicating with patients, delivering complex medical news with compassion, and truly understanding the humanistic side of medicine sets you apart. I will never forget how you held my hand while delivering anxiety-inducing news, offering a profound sense of comfort and solace during some of the most daunting moments. Your ability to blend medical expertise with genuine empathy and care is truly remarkable. To think that our paths may not have crossed if you hadn't made the decision to stay an additional month after completing all your graduation requirements makes me all the more grateful. Your commitment to your patients and your eagerness to continue learning shone brightly during that time. Your unwavering dedication and exceptional understanding made a profound difference, and I will always remember your support with deep gratitude. Thank you from the bottom of my heart.

To my ICU nurses—Laura, Shannon, Cat, Andy, Rachel, and the many others whose names aren't listed here—you are truly gifts from God. You stood by my side through countless terrifying procedures, always with a sense of calmness, focus, and optimism, even in the face of the unknown. Your talent and compassion have been a source of strength for me, and I am deeply grateful for the exceptional care you provided to me and my family. Your patience, kindness, and friendship have left a profound mark on my healing journey. You also supported Dale in ways words can hardly express, offering him the comfort and strength he needed during this time. For all of this and more, I am eternally thankful.

To my team of speech pathologists, I can't imagine the stress and pressure you were under treating a fellow SLP, but I am grateful you were by my side every step of the way. I know many of the conversations we shared were challenging, but I appreciated your dedication and patience. Lindsey and Danielle, thank you for helping me speak again. Your unwavering support and knowledge played a crucial role in my recovery, and I am so grateful for your expertise. Sherry, I am grateful for your aggressive approach to getting me eating again and for the unwavering friendship and patience you showed me. Your support extended far beyond the clinical setting; it was a beacon of hope and comfort during a time when I needed it most. Today, your friendship remains a cherished part of my life, and I am continually inspired by your kindness. Your belief in my recovery and your genuine support of both Dale and me have left a lasting impact, and I am deeply thankful for the bond we have developed.

To Dr. Ashley Reed, I appreciate you rising to the challenge, communicating with Dale, and ensuring I was welcomed and properly cared for at Desert Regional Medical Center. Your unwavering commitment to helping me return to work safely and your incredible compassion in guiding me through the mental and physical challenges I faced truly stood out. While I was away from work, I forgot so much, but you went above and beyond by spending an incredible amount of your own time Zooming with me from a distance. Your patience and dedication helped me reacclimate to the working world and remember the intricacies of writing IEP documents that I had long forgotten. Your innate ability to show compassion and support made a world of difference to my family during this challenging time.

To my physical therapists, Jess and Tara, you are both incredible and talented people, full of sunshine and true gifts to your patients. I appreciate your positivity and unwavering support. You pushed and encouraged me to achieve goals that are rarely seen in the ICU setting, and I am deeply grateful for your continued friendship. I love how, no matter where we are living on this planet, we manage to stay connected and keep our friendship alive over the years. Your commitment to staying in touch, sharing in life's moments, and offering your support means more to me than words can express. I am truly touched by your kindness and will always cherish our bond.

To my ICU doctors at UCSD, who worked tirelessly to find a diagnosis and develop a plan of care for me. I appreciate your dedication to exploring every option, your persistence in the face of uncertainty, and your unwavering commitment to my recovery. Your expertise and determination were instrumental in guiding us through this challenging journey.

To my PICS support group friends, I want to express my deepest gratitude for always being there to listen—to my fears, my worries, and all the moments when I've poured my heart out. Your suggestions and advice have been a guiding light through some of the most challenging times in my life. Your encouragement and friendship have been invaluable. Even in moments when I was crying, feeling vulnerable, and ashamed, you made me feel understood and supported, which has made a profound difference in my life. I am incredibly grateful to call you friends, and for the profound impact you've had on my life. Thank you for being a part of it and for coming into my life when I needed it the most.

To Dr. Amy Bellinghausen and social workers Dr. Jessica Noble and Anna Lewis, thank you for shedding light on ICU survivors and for your tireless dedication to improving my life post-ICU. Your compassion, expertise, and support have been invaluable in my recovery journey. I deeply appreciate your guidance in navigating the depression and anxiety that plagued me during my recovery, helping me find hope and strength when I needed it most.

To Janet and James, my physical trainers, I appreciate your skill set, knowledge base, and expertise. Janet, thank you for your coaching on nutrition and for never giving up on me, even when I came into your office feeling depressed, suicidal, and unmotivated. James, I am grateful that you introduced me to the Neubie and the power of direct current electrical stimulation. You both transformed my life and body, helping me regain physical strength and restore the crucial brain-body connection. Your dedication and personalized approach have been instrumental in rebuilding my physical resilience and overall well-being. I am profoundly thankful for the positive changes you've brought to my health, and for helping me achieve a level of strength I once thought was out of reach.

To Dr. Jeremy Moffit and Dr. Eric Davenport at Gonstead Family Chiropractic, thank you for your unwavering support and expert care. Your exceptional skill set and deep knowledge in treating the whole person, along with your willingness to help me on weekends and after hours, and to make hospital visits when I was in such a critical state, demonstrated your profound dedication to improving the lives of your patients. I'll never forget all you did for me.

And to all those medical professionals that I did not mention but were there by my side supporting me, working tirelessly to provide care, comfort, and hope to me and countless other patients: I'm at a loss for how to express my gratitude for all you give to me and others. Thank you for your selflessness, your expertise, and your unwavering dedication to others' health and well-being. Your kindness and compassion carried me through moments of profound terror and fear. Your support was a guiding light during our darkest times, and I will always be deeply grateful for the extraordinary impact you had on my life. Your expertise and kindness have profoundly changed me and the way I live my life.

To my dear friends and colleagues who drove me to therapy appointments, assisted with daily tasks like washing and drying my hair, took my child to school, organized after-school playdates so I could rest, provided unwavering support and encouragement to my family, and helped me transition back into the working world. I am deeply grateful that you know what it means to be a true friend. Your selflessness, kindness, and generosity have touched my heart in ways words cannot fully express. Thank you for being there when I needed you most.

To my extended family and distant relatives, thank you for the support and encouragement you gave us from afar. Your love and support surely did not go unnoticed. Thank you for helping to watch our daughter, sending cards, and countless text messages offering words of support and love during this difficult period. You taught us that even from afar, the bond of family is a powerful source of comfort and strength, reminding us that we are never truly alone in our struggles.

To the staff and membership at BIGHORN Golf Club, I am so deeply grateful to you all. You exceeded all expectations with your incredible support and generosity. Your willingness to go above and beyond, providing care and resources, was a true testament to your character. Thank you for working out alongside me, offering to drive me to appointments, encouraging me, and supporting my family like you did. I can never express the deep and immense gratitude I have for each and every one of you. I am beyond humbled by the overwhelming kindness, generosity, and sense of community you all have shown me.

Thank you, Dr. Maron, for your unwavering guidance and expertise throughout my medical journey. Your knowledge and compassion provided immense comfort during such a terrifying time. You were a constant source of support for Dale, continually reviewing my medical records and offering invaluable advice that helped guide our decisions. Your dedication and accessibility reassured us during moments of uncertainty, and your involvement made a tremendous difference in my care. I am forever grateful for your compassionate presence and the crucial role you played in my recovery.

To Dr. Marie Pinizzotto and Dr. Carol Ammon, your presence and support were constant throughout this challenging journey. You gave so selflessly of your time, resources, and knowledge, always with my best interests at heart, and never expecting anything in return. Your commitment to my recovery and your generosity in sharing your expertise were invaluable. You helped us navigate through uncertainty and fear, ensuring I could reach my fullest potential in healing. Your unwavering dedication and kindness made all the difference, and I am deeply thankful for your support. Thank you from the bottom of my heart.

To Britton Murrey, my growth strategy coach, your encouragement, positivity, and remarkable ability to understand both me and my vision for growing a business that helps others is truly astounding. Our Zoom meetings were not just productive but inspiring, and I always left our sessions feeling more confident, organized, and motivated to pursue my goals. Your guidance has been invaluable, and your unwavering belief in my potential has made all the difference. Thank you for being a source of inspiration, for your insightful advice, and for helping me turn my dreams into reality. (Find him at www.unboundstrategy.co)

To my dear readers, this book is also for you. Your interest and support have given me the courage to share my story. Thank you for taking the time to read these pages and for joining me on this journey. May you find inspiration in the triumphs, strength in the struggles, and hope in the moments of vulnerability shared within these words. My hope is that you never feel alone in your own journey and that my story reminds you that we are all connected through our experiences. Your journey as a reader makes this journey as an author worthwhile. I am deeply grateful for each one of you.

This dedication has grown lengthy because I wanted to acknowledge everyone who played a significant role in my recovery. It took a month to write this section, and though you may not be listed by name, your support is no less appreciated. Please know that, with tremendous gratitude, I had to bring this to a close eventually. To all the unnamed cheerleaders, experts, friends, and everyone else who helped me along the way—thank you. Your contributions, both big and small, have made a profound impact on my journey and, while not mentioned, are not forgotten.

And lastly, most importantly, to my precious little daughter. At such a young age, you have unknowingly become the greatest source of inspiration and motivation in my life to recover. Writing this to you has been a deeply emotional journey, filled with moments of struggle and reflection. I fought hard through every challenge and setback, never wanting to let you down. I poured my heart into becoming the mom you deserve, and every step of this journey has been driven by my love for you. I love you always and forever, sweet girl. This book is dedicated to you with all my love and admiration as a testament to the incredible journey we've shared and the endless possibilities that lie ahead. May it inspire you to dream big, pursue your passions with unwavering determination, and always believe in yourself. Never give up, even when the road ahead feels impossible. Your strength and joy have been a constant source of light and motivation, and I am endlessly proud of the person you are becoming. I love you to the moon and back—always and forever.

www.ingramcontent.com/pod-product-compliance
Lightning Source LLC
Chambersburg PA
CBHW070532090426
42735CB00013B/2953